Global Outreach
Cookbook

Lahey Clinic

The Lahey Clinic Global Outreach Cookbook
contains recipes gathered from Lahey Clinic physicians,
support staff, alumni, trustees, patients, friends, and
many of our favorite restaurants. The Global Outreach
Program, through the sale of this cookbook, will make it
possible for Lahey Clinic personnel to expand their
commitment to people helping people.

This cookbook is a collection of our favorite recipes,
which are not necessarily original recipes.

Published by Lahey Clinic and produced by:
Favorite Recipes® Press
an imprint of

FRP

P.O. Box 305142
Nashville, Tennessee 37230
1-800-358-0560

Library of Congress Number: 93-071223
ISBN: 0-87197-371-5

Printed in the United States of America
First Printing: 1993 6,000 copies
Second Printing: 2000 3,000 copies

Contents

Acknowledgments

Project Coordinators: Patricia A. Newton
Lisa G. Polacke

Copy Editors: Patricia J. Jacobs
Pauline R. Katz
T. Richardson Miner, Jr.

Front Cover Design: James Millerick
Lisa G. Polacke

Back Cover Design: Wayne Morrell
Rockport, MA

Art Consultants: Kate Bird
Ann Goolkasian

Photography Consultant: R. J. Chevalier

Culinary Consultants: James F. Connolly, C.W.C.
Executive Chef at Lahey Clinic
Michael O'Connor
Sous Chef at Lahey Clinic

Special Support: Joseph H. Bowlds, M.D.
Ophthalmology
David J. Bryan, M.D.
Plastic and Reconstructive Surgery
Patricia L. Eby, M.D.
Plastic and Reconstructive Surgery
David T. Martin, M.D.
Cardiology
Sarkis H. Soukiasian, M.D.
Ophthalmology

Support Staff: Lola Daigle — Becky McMenimen
Mary DeChiara — Charlotte Melillo
Renee Emmonds — Elise Newton
Jo Fernandez — Sheila Shannon
Helen Fram — Virginia Strazzulla
Melanie MacDonald — Polly Zorolow
Kelly Maloney

The Lahey Clinic

Pictured: Lahey Clinic, Kenmore Square; Frank H. Lahey, M.D.

*L*ahey Clinic was founded in Boston in 1923 by world-famous surgeon Frank H. Lahey, M.D., who resigned from his academic positions at Tufts and Harvard Medical Schools to devote himself to clinical practice. Dr. Lahey invited three physicians, Lincoln F. Sise, M.D., Sara M. Jordan, M.D., and Howard M. Clute, M.D., along with M. Blanche Wallace, R.N., to make up the nucleus of an innovative team approach to medicine, beginning a commitment to provide quality, comprehensive health care for all patients who came to the Lahey Clinic from New England and around the world.

From the beginning, the Lahey Clinic medical staff achieved an international reputation in the fields of thyroid, liver and biliary tract surgery, radiation therapy for cancer, urology and diagnostic imaging. Sara M. Jordan, M.D., was one of the leading gastroenterologists of her time. Over the years, the number of patients who came to the Clinic from throughout the world continued to increase dramatically, and in 1980, the Clinic moved to the Boston suburb of Burlington and opened its hospital and outpatient clinic facility.

Lahey Clinic is a comprehensive diagnostic and treatment center committed to the highest level of patient care. While providing this level of specialty care, Lahey Clinic is also a primary care center dedicated to meeting all of the health needs of its patients. To achieve this high standard of care, the Clinic has developed a multispecialty team approach to the delivery of services.

Lahey Clinic is also a teaching institution. Every year, approximately 75 young physicians participate in postgraduate training programs in 30 specialties, including such specialties as diagnostic radiology, colon and rectal surgery, endocrinology, and neurology.

Section of Cardiology, Fellows and Staff, Lahey Clinic, 1992

Lahey Clinic has an active Alumni Association that includes more than 1,900 physicians throughout the world who have received extensive specialized training from members of the professional medical staff.

The Clinic's vision of clinical excellence is further enhanced by its commitment to a leadership role in developing innovative treatments and participating in landmark research.

Today the Clinic has a full-time salaried medical staff of 300 physicians who see nearly 3,000 outpatients a day and more than 500,000 patients a year for treatment of problems ranging from the common cold to rare types of cancer. A 272-bed acute-care hospital includes medical and surgical intensive care units and a cardiac care unit. The inpatient care provided at Lahey—where delicate brain surgery, kidney transplants and open-heart surgery are common—ranks among the most complex in the United States.

Lahey Clinic is constantly reaching out not only to its surrounding communities but also to the larger community that includes the nation and the world.

Lahey physicians have long been interested in offering their services to those in the international community, either as faculty members or as officers in international medical societies, or by volunteering to travel to developing countries to provide free medical care to people in need.

To support humanitarian efforts, the Global Outreach Program was established. This program, founded in 1993, funds travel expenses worldwide for Lahey Clinic medical and non-medical personnel who have been accepted to work with charitable organizations providing free medical care. These medical missions last from several days to several weeks.

Lahey staff has traveled to Armenia, Bolivia, Cambodia, Colombia, Cuba, Ecuador, El Salvador, Haiti, India, Nepal, Paraguay, Peru, St. Lucia, South Africa and Venezuela.

Participants have included members of the departments of Cardiology, Colon and Rectal Surgery, Gastroenterology,

Primitive conditions in El Salvador where people are very much in need of services

Lahey Clinic Ophthalmologist, Joseph H. Bowlds, M.D., (center) is honored by Drs. Alan Gruber and Vicki Guzman for his participation in the Eye Program in El Salvador.

General Surgery, Nursing, Ophthalmology, Orthopaedic Surgery, Physical Therapy, and Plastic and Reconstructive Surgery.

Dr. Joseph H. Bowlds, a Lahey Clinic ophthalmologist, just completed his eleventh medical mission to El Salvador in January 2000. Accompanying him to the rural town of Santa Ana were nine members of the Clinic's ophthalmology department. The team worked over twelve hours a day and treated between 1200 and 1400 patients in a week. Eyesight testing and treatment for cataracts, glaucoma and strabismus occupied most of their time as well as surgical procedures performed on about five percent of the patients they examined.

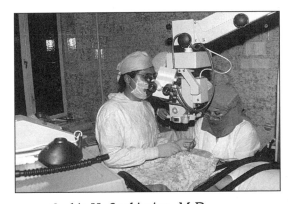

Sarkis H. Soukiasian, M.D., performing surgery in Armenia

Although conditions are not optimal and the physicians must make do with what instruments they have, Dr. Bowlds states, "I have gained a great deal of personal satisfaction bringing some health care to people who wouldn't get it otherwise."

In June and October 1999, Anne Reilly, certified nurse practitioner from Lahey Holliston Pediatrics, traveled to Romania to assist at an orphanage in the town of Brasov. A grant from the Global Outreach Program made it possible for her to care for abandoned children and teach the staff on crucial developmental issues.

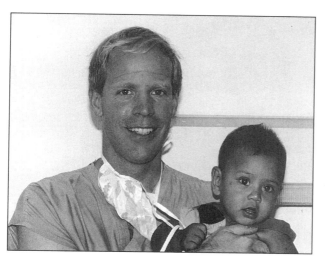

As Anne recalls, "Two hundred and fifty children, newborn through age three, reside at the orphanage. The staff is loving but can only provide limited custodial care due to lack of staffing.

David J. Bryan, M.D., with
young patient in Mexico

A young boy prior to surgery
with his mother in Ecuador

The infants especially are rarely cuddled or held, and often spend hours in the cribs soaked in wet bedding. The lack of stimulation was apparent in some children's blank gazes, rocking motions or autistic-like hand movements. The toddlers are especially starved for affection, because they will charge at you as a group crying, 'Mama, Mama' begging to be picked up. The children rarely go outside to play and the playground that is next to the dumpster

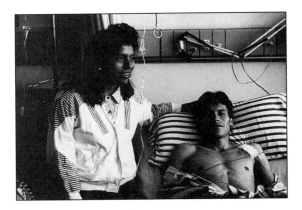

A 29-year-old agricultural engineer from rural Bolivia pictured with his sister after pacemaker implantation. Prior to the operation, the patient was disabled by complete heart block due to Chagas' disease (parasitic infestation of the heart muscle) and was unable to work. After surgery he returned to his job advising farmers on the most productive uses of their land.

consists of concrete and a few broken swings."

All Global Outreach participants have agreed that the medical missions are a life-changing event.

"This trip to Romania has had an immense impact on my life," Reilly says. "This trip was a gift from God to be able to visit and be with these children. The blessings and love the children gave back to us will never be forgotten."

For more information on the Lahey Clinic Global Outreach program, please call the Philanthropy Office at (781) 744-3333.

Let Us Celebrate

*Let us celebrate
The spirit of
Reaching high,
As we spread our wings
And fly
To heights unknown.
Let us be proud together,
As brothers and sisters
In far-off lands.
Faces we cannot see,
Yet, in our hearts
We can hold hands.
Let us rejoice
As we connect
With one another.
Each year, each day
As the spirit moves us,
We will find our way.*

Pauline Katz
January 1993

Contributors

Anne Abbruzzese
Richard V. Abdo, M.D.
Denise Haley Abplanalp
Rosalyn Adams
Marian Adderley
Sharon E. Alexander
Susana R. Alvarez, M.D.
Judith Avery
Martha Baer
Julie Balaban
Nancy Barbeau
Norma E. Bassett
John and Kazuko Beamis
Harriet Bennett
Arlene F. Berg
Elaine Bergeron
Marzina C. Bockler
Angel Bova
Gail V. Bowlds
Nancy Braasch
Florence L. Brackett
Rebecca Bradley, M.S., R.D.
Christine M. Brandt, R.N.
Patty Brent
David J. Bryan, M.D.
Cynthia A. Bryant
Celeste Buckley
Kathryn Burke
James P. Burke, M.D.
Ellen Byda
Susan Cain
Donald Cappadona, M.D.
Lee M. Cappucci
Eva L. Carlson
Karen Carney
Dayle Caterino
Leatrice Chafetz
Dimitria P. Chakalis
Bill Chapin
Rick Chevalier
James F. Connolly, C.W.C.
Lynn Connors
Gretchen Stone Cook
Lucie-Anne Cormier
Arlene Coughlin
Betty Crogan

Jeanne Croland
Barbara J. Cross
Natalie Daddario
Lola Daigle
Grace E. Dare
Sara R. Davies-Lepie, M.D.
Alice G. Davis
Barbara Davison
Mr. & Mrs. A.R. de Arellano
Mary C. DeChiara
Francine DeFrancesco
Ann DeVito
Dorothy Dembowski
Rona P. DiPietro
Jeanne Doherty
Joan Donahue
Anne Drinkwater
Helen Drover
Gloria DuPont
Carol Baffi Dugan
Sandy Duggan
Joanne Duncan
Mimi G. Duncan
Mary V. Dunmore
Patricia Eby, M.D.
Gertrude M. Eckert
Barbara Elkind
Gary & Renee Emmonds
Marion C. Empsall
Charles A. Fager, M.D.
Jo Fernandez
Ruth Fillmore
Ellen Fishman
Martha S. Fleming
Susan S. Foley
Pierre Forgacs, M.D.
Ann Foster
Susan S. Frary
Jean Fraser
Helen Freidberg
Mr. & Mrs. William Frith
Elizabeth H. Galbraith
Mrs. James M. Gavin
Evans Gazala
Susan Cammer Gerstein
Alyshia Gibbs

Mary Gifford
Midge Giodano
Mrs. Robert Goldman
Pamela Gossman
Carolyn Gould
Judithanne Gray
Beverley Guerard
Lynne Gundersen
José A. Gutrecht, M.D.
Elizabeth Haker
Terry Hale
Bill Hamilton
G. Frances Hansen
Veronica Hatfield
Valerie Heemstra
Ann C. Heffernon
Barbara Heiss
Maizie S. Hescock
Jacqueline Hetnik
Lori Hicks
Rose E. Hines
Ann Hogg
Eloise Houghton
Jane Hughes
Kerry J. Hughes
Betty Hunt
Pam Hurlbert
Margaret M. Hurley
Lauren Hutton
Mary Ellen Iorio
Sylvia Izen
Karen L. Jackson
Rosita Japlit
Kala Joblon & Stan
    Mickelson
Marlene E. Johansen
Winona D. Jones
Ruth Joslyn
Genevieve V. Kacmarczyk
Kassie Kattwinkel
Pauline Katz
Peggy Kelley
Anne Kennedy
Barbara Kess
Aabroo I. Khawaja
Kay Klimarchuk

Contributors

Glenn B. Knight, Ph.D.
Barbara Krey
Chris & Carol Kuhn
Eleanor & John Lamont
Beth Landry
Sue Landry
Maxwell Lazinger, M.D.
Maribeth Leahy
Jay Leno
Mary Jo Libertino
Eva Litten
Doris E. Ludlam
Marie C. Ludwick
Vivian A. Lukas
Dolores Macaulay
Melanie F. MacDonald
Bill MacKay
Muriel J. MacKenzie
Sandy Magerer
Terry Maggiore
Nancy Makarowski
Carol Maloney
Kelly Maloney
Cathy Mandel
Frances Mannino
Diane Marasca
Bev Marotto
David T. Martin, M.D.
Betsy Mazzoleni
Mrs. G.W.F. McCain
Mrs. John L. McCrea
Dorothy McCulloch
Marie G. McDonough
Mary T. McGinnis
Robert F. McLellan
Rebecca F. McMenimen
Fran McNeeley
Charlotte Melillo
Fern Meyers
Shawn P. Middleton
Olive Milgate
John Mills
T. Richardson Miner, Jr.
Carol Morrell
G. Virginia Murphy
Richard Murray

Russell Ward Nadeau
Patricia A. Newton
Nancy Nichols
Brenda Nieh
Ethel O'Connor
Winnie Ooi, M.D.
Ronald W. Owen
Terri Palmer
Lucia Palmer, M.D.
Michail & Elena Pankratov
August C. Paoli
Elaine M. Pfeifer
Sheryl L. Pike
Betsy Plummer
Lisa G. Polacke
Barbara Porter
Rachel L. Pouliot
Dolores Pranowski
Ardys M. Proctor
Mrs. Myron Purdy
Deborah Quigley
Michelle Redmond, R.N.
Mrs. Pendennis W. Reed
Brenda Reilly
Warren Rhodes
Mary Richards
Mrs. William G.
  Richeimer, Sr.
Roberta M. Robinson
Sara K. Robinson
Mark P. Roche
Carol Russell
Lynne Sallinger
Karen Sanderson
Grace M. Sargent
Margaret Satterly
Mary Jane Scholz
John G. Shaheen
David & Mary Shahian
Lois Shand
Sheila A. Shannon
Elaine Shaunessy
Mark L. Silverman, M.D.
Claire M. Simas
Ronni Sinclair
Dorothy E. Smerdon

Leigh Smith, R.N.
Sarkis & Linda
  Soukiasian
James T. Sparks, M.D.
Carol Spencer
Diane Spencer
Donna Spencer
Priscille St. Louis
Allison Stange
Phyllis Steinberg
Sharon Steinberg
Gillian Steinhauer
Margaret Stepanian
Margaret Stetler
Virginia R. Strazzulla
Carol Strudas
Patty Sumner
Neil & Elizabeth
  Swinton
Donna Takacs
Karen T.G. Tanzer
William L. Tanzer, O.D.
J. Philip Teixeira
Mariette Theriault
Christine B.
  Thomas, M.D.
Martha E. Thornton
Kathleen A. Timony
Sylvia Tolman
Patricia Toye
Judy Trant
Sheila Veidenheimer
Ana Gregoria Vila
Mrs. Peter Volpe
Carol Von Ette
Elaine Weiner
Claire Wilson, M.D.
Mrs. Robert E. Wise
Beverly Woodford
Hillary Wright, R.D.
Carl Wrubel
Brenda Zielinski
Vinnie Zinna
Mrs. Morton Zuckerman

Restaurants

THE
BAY TOWER
ROOM

Linguine with Smoked Salmon in Caper Cream Sauce

1 pound uncooked fresh linguine
8 ounces shiitake mushrooms, sliced
8 ounces snow peas
1/4 cup finely chopped red bell pepper
2 tablespoons olive oil
3 tablespoons capers
2 ounces white wine
1 cup unsalted butter, chopped
8 ounces smoked salmon, chopped
Salt and pepper to taste

Cook linguine *al dente* using package directions; drain and keep warm. Sauté mushrooms, snow peas and bell pepper in olive oil in large sauté pan for 1 to 2 minutes. Stir in capers and wine. Cook until liquid is reduced by 1/2; reduce heat. Stir in butter. Combine with salmon and linguine in bowl; toss to mix well. Season with salt and pepper. Serve with crisp cheese croutons or breadsticks. Yield: 4 appetizer servings.

The Bay Tower Room
Boston, Massachusetts

Bishop's restaurant, inc. _____

Stuffed Grape Leaves

100 fresh grape leaves
1 cup uncooked rice
1½ pounds ground lamb
Juice of 1 lemon
½ teaspoon each cinnamon, allspice and pepper
1 tablespoon salt
Juice of 1 lemon

Rinse grape leaves. Combine with warm water in bowl. Let stand until flexible. Combine rice, lamb, juice of 1 lemon and seasonings in bowl; mix well. Spoon about 1 tablespoonful lamb mixture in a line across veined side of each grape leaf. Fold in sides and roll to enclose filling. Line bottom of saucepan with additional grape leaves. Arrange rolls in layers in prepared saucepan. Place inverted plate on top of rolls. Add water to level of plate. Bring to a boil; reduce heat. Simmer, covered, for 20 to 30 minutes or until cooked through. Add juice of remaining lemon just before removing from heat. May use bottled grape leaves. Yield: 10 servings.

Bishop's Restaurant, Inc.
Lawrence, Massachusetts

THE BOSTONIAN HOTEL
AT FANEUIL HALL MARKETPLACE

Maine Crab Cakes

1 medium red onion, finely chopped
1 tablespoon oil
1/2 cup red wine vinegar
1 pound Maine crab meat
3 cups white bread crumbs, toasted
1 tablespoon chopped parsley
1 teaspoon Worcestershire sauce
1 teaspoon Tabasco sauce
1/4 teaspoon salt
1/8 teaspoon pepper
1 tablespoon oil

Sauté onion in 1 tablespoon oil in heavy skillet over medium heat until tender and light brown. Add vinegar. Cook until vinegar is reduced enough to just coat onions; remove from heat. Combine with crab meat, bread crumbs, parsley, Worcestershire sauce, Tabasco sauce, salt and pepper in bowl; mix well. Shape into cakes 2 inches wide and 1 inch thick. Brown crab cakes a few at a time in 1 tablespoon oil in heavy skillet over medium-high heat. Remove crab cakes to baking sheet as they brown. Bake at 350 degrees for 5 minutes to reheat. Serve with corn salsa, chunky salsa or cocktail sauce. Yield: 10 to 12 crab cakes.

The Bostonian Hotel at Faneuil Hall Marketplace
Boston, Massachusetts

Brennan's

Bananas Foster

4 bananas
¹/₄ cup butter
1 cup packed brown sugar
¹/₂ teaspoon cinnamon
¹/₄ cup banana liqueur
¹/₄ cup rum
4 scoops vanilla ice cream

Slice bananas into halves lengthwise and crosswise. Melt butter in flambé pan over alcohol burner. Stir in brown sugar, cinnamon and liqueur. Heat for several minutes. Stir in rum. Heat for several minutes. Tip pan to allow flame to ignite sauce. Rotate pan over burner until flames subside. Arrange bananas over ice cream in serving dishes. Spoon sauce over top. Yield: 4 servings.

Brennan's Restaurant
New Orleans, Louisiana

The Cafe Budapest

Chicken Paprika

2 medium onions, minced
1 cup chicken fat
2 cloves of garlic, crushed
2 green bell peppers, sliced
2 tomatoes, peeled, chopped
2 chickens, cut up
2 tablespoons Hungarian paprika
1/2 teaspoon crushed red pepper
4 cubes chicken base
2 cups sour cream
1 cup cream
3 tablespoons flour
Salt to taste

Sauté onions in chicken fat in large heavy saucepan over high heat until light brown; reduce heat. Add garlic, green peppers and tomatoes. Sauté until green peppers are tender. Rinse chicken and pat dry. Add to saucepan. Sauté until chicken begins to turn white. Add paprika, red pepper, chicken base and enough water to just cover. Simmer until chicken is cooked through. Remove chicken to platter. Blend sour cream, cream and flour in small bowl, whisking until smooth. Add to sauce. Bring to a boil. Boil for 1 minute, stirring constantly. Season with salt. Strain into serving bowl. Add chicken. Serve with noodles. Yield: 6 servings.

The Café Budapest
Boston, Massachusetts

Beef Stew

4 pounds stew beef
12 cups beef stock
10 ounces tomato purée
1 bay leaf
2 large carrots
2 stalks celery
1 small turnip
1 large Spanish onion
3 large potatoes
1 cup flour
1/2 cup melted butter
Salt and pepper to taste

Roast stew beef in roasting pan at 450 degrees until brown. Combine with beef stock, tomato purée and bay leaf in 8-quart saucepan. Simmer for 1 1/2 hours. Chop carrots, celery, turnip, onion and potatoes into 1-inch pieces. Cook potatoes in water in saucepan until nearly tender; drain. Cook remaining vegetables in water in saucepan until tender but still firm; drain. Blend flour into butter in saucepan. Cook for 3 to 5 minutes or until light brown. Add to stew with vegetables. Cook until thickened and done to taste, stirring occasionally. Season with salt and pepper; discard bay leaf. May omit roux of butter and flour for a thinner stew. Yield: 10 servings.

Bull & Finch Pub
Boston, Massachusetts

Buteco Restaurant

Black Beans

4 cups dried black beans
3 bay leaves   ¹/₂ large onion, chopped
1 tablespoon oil
Chopped garlic, salt and pepper to taste

Soak beans in water to cover overnight; drain. Combine with fresh water to cover and bay leaves in large saucepan. Cook for 1 hour or until tender. Sauté onion in oil in skillet until dark brown. Add garlic, salt and pepper. Cook for several minutes. Add to beans. Cook for 15 minutes; discard bay leaves. Serve with meat, rice and Vegetarian Medley. May process in blender to serve as soup; garnish servings with chopped scallions. Yield: 12 servings.

Vegetarian Medley

2 cups chopped broccoli   2 cups chopped cauliflower
2 cups shredded carrots
2 cups shredded collard greens   ¹/₂ onion, sliced
¹/₂ green bell pepper, sliced
2 tomatoes, sliced   Chopped garlic to taste
¹/₂ teaspoon salt   Pepper to taste
2 tablespoons olive oil   2 cups water

Arrange broccoli, cauliflower, carrots, collard greens, onion, green pepper and tomatoes in a decorative pattern in large skillet. Sprinkle with garlic, salt and pepper. Drizzle with olive oil. Add water. Cook, covered, for 10 minutes; drain. Serve with black beans and rice. Yield: 12 servings.

Buteco Restaurant
Boston, Massachusetts

Cafe
ESCADRILLE

Charred Tuna with Oyster Sauce

8 fresh oysters
2 cloves of garlic, chopped
1 teaspoon chopped fresh ginger
2 tablespoons sesame oil
1 teaspoon molasses
3 tablespoons oyster sauce
1/4 cup rice wine or white wine
Juice of 1/2 lemon
Salt and cayenne pepper to taste
1 teaspoon cornstarch or arrowroot
1/4 cup water
12 to 16 ounces tuna steaks, 1 inch thick
Cajun seasoning to taste

Drain oysters, reserving liquid. Sauté garlic and ginger in sesame oil in saucepan until tender but not brown. Add reserved oyster liquid, molasses, oyster sauce, wine, lemon juice, salt and cayenne pepper. Stir in mixture of cornstarch and water. Cook until thickened, stirring constantly. Add oysters. Cook until edges of oysters begin to curl; keep warm. Season both sides of tuna lightly with Cajun seasoning. Cook in hot skillet for 1 minute on each side or until medium rare. Slice 1/2 inch thick. Arrange slices in fans on 2 serving plates. Spoon oyster sauce over top. Garnish with green onions. Serve with rice and stir-fried vegetables.
Yield: 2 servings.

Café Escadrille
Burlington, Massachusetts

Dandelion Green Restaurant

Toasted Almond Sundae Sauce

³/4 cup packed brown sugar
1 cup Amaretto
1 cup sliced almonds
1 cup butter

Combine brown sugar, Amaretto and half the almonds in bowl; mix well. Heat butter in skillet over medium heat until foamy but not brown. Add remaining almonds. Cook until golden brown, stirring frequently. Add to Amaretto mixture; mix well. Serve over ice cream. Yield: 15 servings.

Dandelion Green Restaurant
Burlington, Massachusetts

DURGIN – PARK RESTAURANT

Yankee Pot Roast

1 rib cap of beef   6 to 8 stalks celery, sliced
1   16-ounce can whole tomatoes in purée
2 onions, chopped   Carrots, sliced
Potatoes, cut into quarters
Celery salt and white pepper to taste

Place beef in roasting pan. Roast at 450 degrees for 1 hour. Combine with water to cover in stockpot. Cook for 2 hours. Add celery, tomatoes, onions, carrots and potatoes. Cook for 1 hour or until vegetables and beef are tender. Season with celery salt and white pepper. Yield: Variable.

Baked Indian Pudding

1 cup yellow cornmeal $1/2$ cup black molasses
$1/4$ cup sugar
$1/4$ teaspoon baking soda
2 eggs $1/4$ cup butter
$1/4$ teaspoon salt
6 cups hot milk

Combine cornmeal, molasses, sugar, baking soda, eggs, butter, salt and half the milk in greased stoneware crock or baking dish. Bake in hot oven for 30 minutes or until mixture bubbles. Stir in remaining milk. Bake in slow oven for 5 to 7 hours or until set. Yield: 8 servings.

Durgin-Park Restaurant
Boston, Massachusetts

The European Restaurant Inc.

Spinach Pie European

2 pounds spinach, chopped
32 ounces prepared pizza dough
2 large cloves of garlic, minced
1/2 cup olive oil
Salt and pepper to taste
4 slices American cheese
1/2 cup olive oil

Cook spinach partially in water in saucepan. Drain and press out excess moisture. Press half the pizza dough over bottom and side of oiled 10-inch pie plate. Combine spinach, garlic, 1/2 cup olive oil, salt and pepper in bowl; mix well. Spread evenly in prepared pie plate. Top with cheese. Stretch remaining dough to fit top of pie; place on pie. Trim and seal edges. Brush top with 1/2 cup olive oil. Bake at 325 degrees for 30 to 40 minutes or until golden brown. Yield: 8 servings.

The European Restaurant Inc.
Boston, Massachusetts

Four Seasons' Noisettes of Lamb with Garlic and Roquefort Potato Croquettes

1   8-rib lamb rack, split, chine bone removed
2 heads of garlic, peeled   1 cup extra-virgin olive oil
2 vine-ripened tomatoes or 4 plum tomatoes
1 pound seasonal mushrooms such as shiitake, chanterelle or oyster
8 ounces French-style green beans
2$1/2$ onions, chopped   1 stalk celery, chopped   1 carrot, chopped
1 cup dry white wine   Salt and pepper to taste
1 ounce each fresh tarragon and chives $1/4$ cup butter

Separate rib bones from meat with boning knife; trim fat from meat. Cook bones in enough water in saucepan to yield 2 cups stock; reserve stock. Cook garlic in olive oil in saucepan over very low heat for 1 hour or until garlic is tender but not brown. Strain olive oil. Blanch tomatoes in boiling water for 10 seconds. Cool in iced water. Peel and chop firm portions, reserving seed and juice for sauce. Sauté mushrooms, green beans, onion, celery and carrot in 1 tablespoon garlic-olive oil in small saucepan for 10 minutes or until light brown. Add reserved tomato seed and juice. Sauté for 2 minutes. Add wine. Cook until reduced by $1/2$. Stir in reserved stock. Simmer for 20 minutes without reducing. Season to taste and strain, reserving sauce and vegetables. Season lamb with salt and pepper. Sear on all sides in 2 tablespoons garlic-olive oil in sauté pan over high heat. Place on rack in roasting pan. Roast at 400 degrees for 12 to 14 minutes or to 105 degrees on meat thermometer. Remove to serving platter. Combine reserved sauce with chopped tomato, tarragon and chives in saucepan. Cook until heated through. Whisk in butter and adjust seasonings. Reheat reserved vegetables as desired. Slice lamb into thick noisettes, allowing 2 per person. Stand noisettes in center of serving plates. Arrange 1 croquette and sautéed mushrooms and green beans around lamb. Sauce the plates. Serve with Roquefort Potato Croquettes. Yield: 4 servings.

Roquefort Potato Croquettes: Fold 2 ounces Roquefort cheese and salt and pepper to taste into 8 ounces riced cooked potatoes. Shape into oval croquettes and freeze until firm. Coat with $1/2$ cup flour. Dip into mixture of 2 beaten eggs and 2 tablespoons chopped chives. Coat with 1 cup Japanese bread crumbs. Fry in 375-degree oil until golden brown.

Four Seasons Hotel
Boston, Massachusetts

STOUFFER BEDFORD GLEN HOTEL

HAVILLAND'S
GRILLE

Pan-Fried Encrusted Swordfish

2 cups bread crumbs
1/4 cup finely crushed pine nuts
1/2 teaspoon each oregano and thyme
1 tablespoon each parsley, salt and pepper
2 thin 7-ounce swordfish filets
1/4 cup flour
4 eggs, beaten
1/4 cup olive oil

Mix bread crumbs, pine nuts, oregano, thyme, parsley, salt and pepper in bowl; mix well. Coat fish with flour, shaking off excess. Dip in eggs; coat with bread crumb mixture. Cook in olive oil in skillet for 2 to 3 minutes on each side or until well browned. Place on lightly oiled baking sheet. Bake at 500 degrees for 3 to 4 minutes. Serve with tartar sauce. Yield: 2 servings.

Havilland's Grille
Stouffer Bedford Glen Hotel
Bedford, Massachusetts

Pear Crisp

1 cup pecan pieces
1 cup flour
1 cup packed light brown sugar
$1/2$ teaspoon cinnamon
$1/8$ teaspoon salt
$1/2$ cup unsalted butter
8 firm Anjou, Bosc or Bartlett pears
2 tablespoons sugar
1 tablespoon flour

Spread pecans on baking sheet. Toast at 350 degrees for 6 to 8 minutes or until light brown. Combine with 1 cup flour, brown sugar, cinnamon and salt in bowl. Cut butter into $1/2$ tablespoon pieces. Rub into pecan mixture until crumbly; set aside. Peel and core pears. Slice $1/2$ inch thick. Toss with sugar and 1 tablespoon flour in bowl. Spread in 6x10-inch baking dish; sprinkle with pecan mixture. Bake at 350 degrees for 1 hour or until bubbly and crisp. Serve warm with whipped cream.
Yield: 6 to 8 servings.

Jasper's
Boston, Massachusetts

Jimmy's Harborside Restaurant, Inc.

Sole Irene with Caviar Sauce

2 medium red onions, sliced
1 teaspoon pickling spices
4 cups white wine
4 cups cream
1¹/₂ pounds butter
1¹/₂ ounces caviar
1 pound smoked salmon
10   8-ounce grey sole filets
2 cups flour
1 cup margarine
2 teaspoons garlic purée
¹/₄ cup lemon juice
2 tablespoons chopped parsley or chives

Combine red onions, pickling spices and wine in sauté pan. Cook until liquid is reduced by ¹/₂. Whisk in cream. Simmer for 4 minutes. Whisk in butter gradually. Fold in caviar; keep warm. Layer salmon on sole filets, covering completely. Roll sole to enclose salmon; secure with wooden picks. Cut into ¹/₄ to ¹/₂-inch slices, securing each with wooden pick. Coat with flour. Sauté in margarine in hot skillet until light brown on both sides. Add garlic purée and lemon juice. Cook for 2 minutes longer. Spoon desired amount of caviar sauce onto serving plates. Arrange sole slices in sauce. Sprinkle with parsley. Yield: 8 servings.

Jimmy's Harborside Restaurant, Inc.
Boston, Massachusetts

The Kernwood at Lynnfield

Breast of Chicken Scampi

2   8-ounce chicken breast filets
¹/₂ cup flour   3 tablespoons butter
3 cloves of garlic, finely chopped
¹/₄ cup Sauterne   Juice of ¹/₂ lemon
2 tablespoons water
1 tablespoon chopped parsley

Rinse chicken and pat dry. Pound with meat mallet to flatten. Coat with flour, shaking off excess. Cook in butter in 10-inch sauté pan until light brown on 1 side. Turn chicken over and add garlic. Sauté until light brown. Add wine, lemon juice and water. Cook for 1 minute longer. Serve chicken over rice pilaf or angel hair pasta. Spoon sauce over top. Sprinkle with parsley. Yield: 2 servings.

Key Lime Pie

4 egg yolks   Grated zest of 3 limes
1   14-ounce can sweetened condensed milk
10 tablespoons fresh lime juice
1   9-inch graham cracker pie shell

Combine egg yolks, lime zest and condensed milk in stainless steel bowl; mix well. Stir in lime juice. Spoon into pie shell. Bake at 350 degrees for 15 minutes. Chill until serving time. Serve with whipped cream; garnish with lime slices. Yield: 8 servings.

The Kernwood at Lynnfield
Lynnfield, Massachusetts

LaGroceria

Timbano Di Pasta with Polpettine

2 slices white bread
1/2 cup milk
8 ounces ground beef
1 clove of garlic, minced
1 egg
2 tablespoons grated Parmesan cheese
1 teaspoon chopped parsley
Salt and pepper to taste
4 cups tomato sauce (your favorite recipe)
1 eggplant
Flour
Olive oil
1   16-ounce package penne, cooked, drained
1 cup shredded mozzarella cheese
1/2 cup grated Romano cheese

Soak bread in milk in bowl; squeeze dry. Combine with ground beef, garlic, egg, Parmesan cheese, parsley, salt and pepper in bowl; mix well. Shape into very small meatballs. Cook in tomato sauce in saucepan until cooked through. Remove meatballs with slotted spoon. Slice eggplant 1/4 inch thick. Coat with flour. Fry in olive oil in skillet until golden brown on both sides. Layer 1/3 of the tomato sauce, 1/3 of the pasta, half the eggplant, half the meatballs, 1/3 of the mozzarella cheese and 1/3 of the Romano cheese in 4-inch deep baking dish. Repeat layers. Top with remaining pasta, Romano cheese, mozzarella cheese and tomato sauce. Bake at 350 degrees for 45 minutes. Yield: 8 servings.

LaGroceria Restaurant
Cambridge, Massachusetts

La Mia Cucina

Philomena's Pudding

**4 cups milk   ¹/₄ to ¹/₃ cup uncooked farina   Salt to taste
4 eggs, beaten   3 cups sugar   1 teaspoon vanilla extract**

Scald milk in saucepan. Stir in farina and salt. Cool to room temperature. Beat eggs with 1 cup sugar by hand until thick. Stir in cooled milk mixture; set aside. Heat 2 cups sugar in saucepan over low heat until bubbly and brown, stirring constantly. Spoon into 1-piece tube pan, tilting pan quickly to coat entire surface and ³/₄ of tube. Spoon in custard mixture. Set in large pan; add ¹/₂ inch hot water. Bake at 375 degrees for 45 to 60 minutes or until set and lightly crusted. Cool on wire rack. Stir in vanilla. Chill overnight. Run dull knife around side of pan and tube. Rotate pan to free custard from side of pan. Place rimmed pan over pan and invert quickly onto plate. Spoon caramel sauce over servings. May also sprinkle with brown sugar and serve with whipped cream. Yield: 12 servings.

Anna's Bracciole

**6   5-ounce veal cutlets   ¹/₄ cup olive oil
2 tablespoons grated Parmesan cheese   2 tablespoons raisins
1¹/₂ tablespoons chopped basil leaves
1¹/₂ to 2 tablespoons chopped mint   Salt and pepper to taste
Bread crumbs   Tomato sauce (your favorite recipe)**

Brush veal generously with olive oil. Combine cheese, raisins, basil and mint in small bowl. Spoon onto cutlets. Sprinkle with salt, pepper and bread crumbs. Roll cutlets tightly to enclose filling. Arrange in baking pan. Top with tomato sauce. Bake at 325 degrees for 1¹/₄ hours. Serve with ravioli or other pasta. Yield: 6 servings.

La Mia Cucina
Woburn, Massachusetts

Le Bellecour

Mediterranean Seafood Chowder

1 large onion, chopped
2 green bell peppers, chopped
1 red bell pepper, chopped
2 stalks celery, chopped
1 pound mushrooms, sliced
1 tablespoon minced garlic
1 teaspoon basil
1 teaspoon oregano
Olive oil
4 cups mixed vegetable juice cocktail
4 cups clam juice
4 cups tomato juice
1 pint (or more) clams, minced
1/4 cup packed brown sugar
1/2 teaspoon cayenne pepper
Tabasco sauce to taste
Salt and black pepper to taste
Cooked fish, scallops, white fish, shrimp and mussels

Sauté onion, bell peppers, celery, mushrooms, garlic, basil and oregano in olive oil in stockpot until tender. Add juices, clams, brown sugar, cayenne pepper, Tabasco sauce, salt and black pepper; mix well. Simmer for 30 to 60 minutes. Add fish, scallops, white fish, shrimp and mussels. Simmer until heated through. Garnish servings with croutons, aioli and grated Parmesan cheese. Make aioli by mixing garlic mayonnaise with paprika or saffron to taste. Yield: 12 servings.

Le Bellecour
Lexington, Massachusetts

LEGAL SEA FOODS, INC.
Restaurants

Warm Cape Cod Farmed Bay Scallops with
Fresh Tomato Extra-Virgin Olive Oil Vinaigrette

2 tablespoons minced garlic
1/4 cup chopped onion
1/4 cup water
1/3 cup balsamic vinegar
1 teaspoon sugar
Salt and pepper to taste
1 cup extra-virgin olive oil
1 1/4 cups finely chopped seeded tomato
1/4 cup chopped parsley
4 dozen scallops in shells
1/2 cup water
Coarsely shredded salad greens

Process garlic, onion, 1/4 cup water, vinegar, sugar, salt and pepper in food processor until smooth. Add olive oil gradually, processing constantly until smooth. Combine with tomato and parsley in bowl; adjust seasonings. Let stand for several hours to blend flavors. Steam scallops in 1/2 cup water in covered saucepan until scallops are cooked through and shells open. Remove and discard top halves of shells. Cut scallops from bottom halves of shells, leaving in shells. Place shells on beds of salad greens on serving plates. Spoon vinaigrette onto scallops. Serve with remaining vinaigrette. Yield: 4 main-course or 8 appetizer servings.

Legal Sea Foods, Inc.
Burlington, Massachusetts

LOCKE·OBER COMPANY
Established 1875

Baked Lobster Savannah

2 cups sliced mushrooms
1 cup chopped green bell pepper
1/4 cup melted butter
1 tablespoon (heaping) Spanish paprika
1 1/2 cups sherry
Salt and pepper to taste
4 cups cream sauce
1/2 cup chopped pimentos
4 3-pound lobsters, cooked, cooled
Grated Parmesan cheese

Sauté mushrooms and green pepper in butter in large saucepan until tender. Stir in paprika and wine. Cook until reduced by 1/2. Season with salt and pepper. Stir in cream sauce and pimentos. Keep warm. Remove claws and knuckles from lobster. Hold lobster with head up. Cut oval opening in shell from tip of tail to base of head. Remove meat from tail, claws and knuckles; reserve tail shells. Chop meat coarsely, discarding intestinal vein and stomach sac near head. Add to sauce; mix well. Simmer for 10 minutes. Spoon into lobster shells; place on baking sheet. Sprinkle with cheese. Bake at 375 degrees for 15 minutes. Yield: 4 servings.

Locke-Ober Café
Boston, Massachusetts

maison
robert

Duck Salad with Wild Rice

1 Long Island duck
1 teaspoon oil
1/2 cup wild rice, cooked
6 scallions, thinly sliced
1/2 cup seedless green grape halves
1/2 cup pecans
Grated zest and juice of 2 oranges
2/3 cup olive oil
1/3 cup sherry vinegar
Salt and pepper to taste

Rinse duck inside and out and pat dry. Sear on all sides in 1 teaspoon oil in Dutch oven. Bake at 450 degrees for 45 minutes. Cool for 30 minutes. Chop into 1/4x2-inch pieces, discarding skin and bones. Combine with rice, scallions, grapes and pecans in bowl. Combine orange zest, orange juice, 2/3 cup olive oil, vinegar, salt and pepper in small bowl; mix well. Add to salad; mix well. Serve at room temperature without chilling.
Yield: 4 servings.

Maison Robert
Boston, Massachusetts

Marriott.

HOTELS · RESORTS · SUITES

Wild Mushroom Soup

2 teaspoons finely chopped garlic
2 teaspoons finely chopped shallots
3 cups coarsely chopped wild mushrooms
5 ounces butter
1 cup flour
8 cups chicken stock
1 cup brandy
1/8 teaspoon tarragon
1/4 teaspoon basil
1/4 teaspoon oregano
2 cups heavy cream
Salt and pepper to taste

Sauté garlic, shallots and mushrooms in butter in saucepan until tender. Stir in flour. Cook for several minutes, stirring constantly. Add chicken stock. Cook until thickened, stirring constantly. Combine brandy, tarragon, basil and oregano in small saucepan. Ignite brandy and allow alcohol to burn off. Stir in cream. Cook until reduced by 1/3. Add to soup. Simmer for 20 to 30 minutes. Season with salt and pepper. May spoon into ovenproof bowls, top with sliced Brie and broil until golden brown. Serve with Caesar salad and a good wine. Yield: 8 servings.

Boston Marriott
Burlington, Massachusetts

Olives

Chargrilled Tuna and Avocado Salad

1 tablespoon chopped fresh rosemary
2 tablespoons chopped fresh basil   2 cloves of garlic, finely chopped
1 teaspoon finely chopped fresh ginger   Grated zest of 1 orange
1 cup olive oil   6   3-ounce tuna steaks
Salt and pepper to taste   1½ avocados
1 pound mesclun or mixed greens   Toasted Corn Vinaigrette

Combine first 6 ingredients in large bowl. Add tuna; toss to coat well. Marinate for 1 hour or longer. Drain tuna; sprinkle with salt and pepper. Grill until charred on all sides. Cut avocados into thirds. Slice diagonally into fans. Place on salad greens on serving plates. Slice each tuna steak into 3 or 4 pieces. Place over avocado. Spoon Toasted Corn Vinaigrette over top. Garnish with cilantro. Yield: 6 servings.

Toasted Corn Vinaigrette

3 or 4 ears of fresh corn   2 to 4 tablespoons olive oil
1 red onion, minced   1 bunch scallions, chopped
1 tablespoon finely chopped ginger
1 clove of garlic, minced   ½ cup balsamic vinegar
Juice of 1 orange   1¾ cups olive oil
2 tablespoons fresh basil   1 tablespoon fresh thyme
1 tablespoon fresh cilantro   Salt and pepper to taste

Cut kernels from ears of corn. Sauté in 2 to 4 tablespoons olive oil in large skillet until brown. Add onion and scallions. Sauté until tender. Stir in ginger and garlic. Sauté for 3 to 5 minutes. Add vinegar and orange juice; remove from heat. Stir in remaining ingredients. Yield: 6 servings.

Olives
Charlestown, Massachusetts

*P*eking
*G*arden

Hot and Sour Soup

5 cups stock
4 ounces lean pork, shredded
1/2 ounce cloud ears, broken into small pieces
1 ounce golden needles, cut into 2-inch pieces
1 ounce bamboo shoots
1 ounce mushrooms, sliced
2 bean curd cakes, sliced into 1/4-inch strips
3/4 teaspoon sugar
1 tablespoon thick soy sauce
1 1/2 teaspoons salt   2 tablespoons cornstarch
1/4 cup water
3 to 4 tablespoons light vinegar
1 to 2 tablespoons hot oil
1 egg, beaten   Sesame oil to taste
2 scallions, chopped

Bring stock to a boil in large stockpot. Add pork, cloud ears, golden needles, bamboo shoots, mushrooms, bean curd, sugar, soy sauce and salt; mix gently. Cook until heated through. Add mixture of cornstarch and water, vinegar and hot oil. Bring to a boil, stirring constantly. Stir in egg. Serve with a dash of sesame oil; top with scallions. Yield: 6 servings.

Peking Garden
Lexington, Massachusetts

Dutch Pea Soup

2 smoked pork hocks or 1 meaty ham bone and 2 fresh pork hocks
1¹/₂ cups chopped celery
2 carrots, shredded
1 cup chopped onion   2 quarts water
¹/₄ cup chopped fresh parsley
¹/₈ teaspoon rosemary, savory and marjoram
1 bay leaf   Salt to taste
1 pound dried split peas
3 quarts water
4 large leeks with 3 inches stem, sliced
12 to 16 ounces kielbasa, sliced
1¹/₂ cups chopped potatoes

Sauté pork in stockpot for several minutes. Add celery, carrots and onion. Sauté for 5 minutes. Stir in 2 quarts water, parsley, rosemary, savory, marjoram, bay leaf and salt. Simmer for 3 to 4 hours or until meat falls from bones. Strain, reserving stock; discard bay leaf. Chill pork and stock. Skim stock. Cut pork into bite-sized pieces, discarding bones. Cook peas, covered, in 3 quarts water in 6-quart saucepan for 45 minutes; drain. Add to stock with pork and leeks in stockpot. Simmer for 2 hours. Purée enough soup to make of desired consistency. Combine with kielbasa and potatoes in stockpot. Cook just until potatoes are tender. May cook pork in pressure cooker for 45 minutes if preferred.
Yield: 8 main-course servings.

Promises To Keep
Derry, New Hampshire

Publick House

Historic Resort

Individual Lobster Pies

$^1/_4$ cup flour
$^1/_4$ cup melted butter
1 pint milk, scalded
1 pint light cream, scalded
1 pound lobster meat
$^1/_4$ cup butter
$^1/_2$ teaspoon paprika
$^1/_3$ cup sherry
Cayenne pepper to taste
1 teaspoon salt
4 egg yolks
$^3/_4$ cup fresh bread crumbs
3 tablespoons crushed potato chips
1 tablespoon grated Parmesan cheese
5 teaspoons melted butter
$^3/_4$ teaspoon paprika

*B*lend flour into $^1/_4$ cup melted butter in saucepan. Cook over low heat for several minutes, stirring constantly. Add hot milk and cream. Cook for 15 minutes, stirring frequently; strain. Sauté lobster in $^1/_4$ cup butter with $^1/_2$ teaspoon paprika in saucepan. Stir in $^1/_4$ cup wine. Cook for 3 minutes. Add cayenne pepper, salt and cream sauce. Stir 4 tablespoons sauce into egg yolks; stir egg yolks into sauce. Cook until thickened, stirring frequently; remove from heat. Stir in remaining wine. Spoon into individual ramekins. Combine bread crumbs, potato chips, cheese, 5 teaspoons butter and $^3/_4$ teaspoon paprika in bowl; mix well. Sprinkle over pies. Bake at 350 degrees for 45 minutes. Yield: 8 servings.

Publick House
Sturbridge, Massachusetts

Finnan Haddie

1 pound smoked haddock
2 cups water
2 cups half and half or skim milk
1/2 cup flour
6 tablespoons melted butter
1 egg (optional)
Salt and white pepper to taste
4 slices bread, crusts trimmed

Poach haddock in water in covered pan for 8 to 10 minutes. Remove fish to platter. Cook stock until reduced to 1/2 cup. Heat half and half in double boiler until very warm. Whisk flour into melted butter in 1 1/2-quart saucepan over medium-low heat. Whisk in hot half and half and fish stock. Cook until thickened, stirring constantly. Whisk 1/4 cup hot mixture into egg; whisk egg into hot mixture. Cook until thickened, stirring constantly. Flake haddock into sauce with salt and white pepper; mix gently. Spoon into 4 greased individual casseroles. Bake at 350 degrees for 10 minutes or until golden brown and bubbly. Cut bread into quarters. Toast in oven. Serve with casseroles. Yield: 4 servings.

Rocktide Inn
Welles and Melanie Steane
Boothbay Harbor, Maine

Ricotta and Spinach Pie

1/2 cup chopped zucchini
1/2 cup chopped mushrooms
1/2 cup chopped green bell pepper
1 tablespoon oil
3 eggs, slightly beaten
1 cup mixed shredded mozzarella cheese, shredded Cheddar cheese
and grated Parmesan cheese
1   10-ounce package frozen chopped spinach, cooked, drained
2 pounds ricotta cheese
1/2 cup chopped ham or cooked sausage
Freshly ground pepper to taste
Olive oil

Sauté zucchini, mushrooms and green pepper in oil in skillet. Combine eggs, mixed cheeses, spinach, sautéed vegetables, ricotta cheese, ham and pepper in order listed in bowl, mixing with wooden spoon. Spoon into buttered 9-inch springform pan. Brush with olive oil. Place on baking sheet. Bake at 325 degrees for 45 minutes or until knife comes out clean. Let stand for several minutes before removing side of pan. Serve with tomato and basil salad and crusty bread as main course or side dish. Yield: 8 to 12 servings.

Rosalie's Restaurants
Marblehead and Sudbury, Massachusetts

Clam Chowder

1 pound potatoes, peeled, chopped
32 ounces clam juice   2 pounds fresh or frozen clams, chopped
2 ounces salt pork, chopped   1 small onion, chopped
1/2 cup butter   1/2 cup flour   2 cups half and half
Worcestershire sauce, Tabasco sauce, salt and pepper to taste

Bring potatoes and clam juice to a boil in saucepan. Cook until potatoes are tender. Add clams with any juice. Simmer until clams are tender; do not overcook. Remove skin from salt pork. Render in saucepan. Add onion. Cook until onion is tender. Add butter. Cook until melted. Stir in flour. Cook until light brown. Add to chowder. Bring to a boil, stirring constantly. Heat half and half in saucepan. Add enough half and half to chowder to make of desired consistency. Season to taste. Serve with oyster crackers or pilot crackers. Yield: 8 servings.

Corn Bread

3 cups cornmeal   3 cups flour   3/4 cup sugar
1/4 cup baking powder   1 1/2 teaspoons salt
2 1/2 cups milk   1/2 cup eggs
3/4 cup melted shortening

Mix cornmeal, flour, sugar, baking powder and salt in mixer bowl. Add milk, eggs and shortening; beat at medium speed for 30 seconds, scraping bowl. Spoon into greased 18x26-inch baking pan. Bake in hot oven until golden brown. Yield: 24 servings.

Union Oyster House
Boston, Massachusetts

Veal à la Dray

1 medium onion, chopped   1 tablespoon butter
8 ounces mushrooms, chopped   4 artichoke hearts, chopped
4   4x6-inch rectangles puff pastry   4 slices Swiss cheese
4   4-ounce veal cutlets   1 egg, beaten

Sauté onion in butter until tender. Add mushrooms and artichokes. Cook until vegetables are tender. Cool to room temperature. Spoon onto puff pastry rectangles. Layer cheese on veal cutlets; roll veal to enclose cheese. Place rolls on pastry. Brush egg around edges of pastry. Fold pastry over rolls; press edges with fork to seal. Brush with egg. Place on baking sheet. Bake at 400 degrees for 15 to 20 minutes or until golden brown. Serve with Bearnaise Sauce. Yield: 4 servings.

Iced Cherry Soup

1 pound dark sweet cherries, pitted   3/4 cup sugar
2 cups red wine   Juice of 1/2 lemon   2 bay leaves
1/2 teaspoon each cinnamon, nutmeg and ground cloves
2 tablespoons brandy   2 cups sour cream   1/4 cup light cream

Combine cherries, sugar, wine, lemon juice, bay leaves, cinnamon, nutmeg and cloves in saucepan. Cook for 10 minutes. Add brandy. Press through sieve or strainer into bowl. Chill to 40 degrees. Add sour cream and cream; mix well. Chill for several hours. Discard bay leaves. Garnish with whole cherries. Serve as appetizer or between-course palate cleanser. Yield: 6 to 8 servings.

Versailles Restaurant
Lexington, Massachusetts

Appetizers
&
Beverages

Jay Leno's Uncle Louie's Chicken Wings Marinara

2 to 3 dozen chicken wings
Olive oil
Crushed garlic to taste
1   16-ounce can Italian plum
**   tomatoes**
Salt to taste
Several teaspoons chopped parsley
2 tablespoons (or more) Durkee's
**   hot sauce**
Garlic powder

Cook chicken wings by broiling or coat lightly with flour and fry in safflower or peanut oil. While they are cooking prepare the sauce. Pour olive oil into saucepan to 1-inch depth. Season with garlic. Heat for several minutes. Press tomatoes through sieve. Add to oil. Add salt and parsley. Simmer for 20 minutes, stirring frequently. Add hot sauce (a little or a lot, depending on how hot or mild your taste), but put in at least 2 tablespoons or the sauce won't be tasty. Add a little garlic powder. Simmer for 3 or 4 minutes longer, stirring frequently. Pour 1/2 cup sauce in large bowl. Add chicken wings, tossing to coat. Serve with remaining sauce on the side to dip the wings into. Enjoy! Yield: 2 to 3 dozen.

Chinese Chicken Wings

1¹/₂ pounds chicken wings, rinsed
1¹/₂ teaspoons salt
¹/₄ teaspoon pepper
1 teaspoon sugar
¹/₂ cup soy sauce
1 tablespoon ginger
¹/₃ cup sesame oil
Juice of 1 lemon

Cut wings into 3 sections, discarding tips. Mix remaining ingredients in shallow bowl. Add chicken wings, stirring to coat. Chill, covered, for 3 days, turning often. Bake, uncovered, at 350 degrees for 15 minutes or until tender. Broil for 10 minutes or until brown. Yield: 10 servings.

💜 **Approx Per Serving:** Cal 223; Prot 14 g; Carbo 2 g; Fiber <1 g; T Fat 17 g; 70% Calories from Fat; Chol 44 mg; Sod 1185 mg.

Jeanne Doherty, Massachusetts

Rose's Chicken Wings

5 pounds chicken wings, rinsed, disjointed, tips discarded
1 16-ounce bottle Russian dressing
1 envelope onion soup mix
1 16-ounce jar apricot jam

Place chicken in 8x10-inch baking pan. Add mixture of remaining ingredients. Chill, covered, for 8 hours, turning often. Bake at 325 degrees for 1¹/₂ hours. Yield: 40 servings.

💜 **Approx Per Serving:** Cal 211; Prot 12 g; Carbo 9 g; Fiber <1 g; T Fat 14 g; 60% Calories from Fat; Chol 44 mg; Sod 150 mg.

Diane Spencer, Massachusetts

Crabbies

¹/₂ cup butter, softened
1 5-ounce jar Old English cheese spread, softened
1¹/₂ teaspoons mayonnaise
1 teaspoon garlic salt
7 ounces crab meat
6 English muffins, split

Mix first 4 ingredients in bowl. Add crab meat; mix well. Spread on muffins. Place on freezer tray. Store, wrapped, in freezer. Cut into eighths; place on baking sheet. Broil until brown and bubbly. Yield: 40 servings.

💜 **Approx Per Serving:** Cal 59; Prot 2 g; Carbo 4 g; Fiber <1 g; T Fat 4 g; 56% Calories from Fat; Chol 14 mg; Sod 184 mg.

Cynthia A. Bryant, Massachusetts

Gourmet Crab Spread

1 envelope unflavored gelatin
3 tablespoons cold water
1   10-ounce can cream of celery
    soup
6 ounces cream cheese, softened
1 medium onion, finely chopped
1   7-ounce can crab meat
1 cup chopped celery
1/2 cup chopped green olives
1 cup mayonnaise

Soften gelatin in cold water. Heat celery soup in saucepan to boiling point. Remove from heat. Stir in gelatin until dissolved. Add cream cheese, onion, crab meat, celery, olives and mayonnaise; mix well. Pour into 2 oiled medium gelatin molds. Chill until set. Unmold onto serving plate. Garnish with additional olives. Serve with crackers. Yield: 24 servings.

💜 **Approx Per Serving:** Cal 115; Prot 3 g; Carbo 2 g; Fiber <1 g;
   T Fat 11 g; 84% Calories from Fat; Chol 22 mg; Sod 280 mg.

Ronni Sinclair, Georgia

Sugared Baked Brie

1/4 cup packed brown sugar
1/4 cup chopped walnuts
1 tablespoon brandy
1   14-ounce round Brie cheese

Combine brown sugar, walnuts and brandy in bowl; mix well. Chill in refrigerator for up to 1 week. Place cheese in casserole. Bake at 500 degrees for 4 to 5 minutes or until cheese is slightly softened. Sprinkle with brown sugar mixture. Bake for 2 to 3 minutes longer or until brown sugar is melted and cheese is heated through but not melted. Serve with fruit and crackers. Yield: 16 servings.

💜 **Approx Per Serving:** Cal 113; Prot 5 g; Carbo 5 g; Fiber <1 g;
   T Fat 8 g; 64% Calories from Fat; Chol 25 mg; Sod 158 mg.

Ann Hogg, Massachusetts

Hummus bi Tahina

1 cup tahina (sesame seed pureé)
5 cloves of garlic
1   16-ounce can chick-peas, drained
3/4 cup lemon juice
3 tablespoons olive oil
1 teaspoon salt
1/2 to 1 cup water

Combine tahina, garlic, chick-peas, lemon juice, olive oil and salt in food processor container. Process with steel blades until mixture is smooth. Continue processing while adding water until of desired consistency. Chill in refrigerator for 1 hour or longer. Serve with pieces of pita bread. Yield: 40 servings.

💜 **Approx Per Serving:** Cal 61; Prot 2 g; Carbo 4 g; Fiber 1 g; T Fat 5 g; 64% Calories from Fat; Chol 0 mg; Sod 89 mg.

James T. Sparks, M.D., Massachusetts

Herbed Liver Pâté

1 cup finely chopped onions
1/2 cup butter
1 pound chicken livers
1 bay leaf
1 teaspoon salt
1/2 teaspoon pepper
1/2 teaspoon thyme
1/2 teaspoon oregano
1/4 cup butter, softened
2 teaspoons brandy

Sauté onions in 1/2 cup butter in skillet until tender. Remove with slotted spoon; place in blender container. Trim chicken livers; cut each into 3 pieces. Add chicken livers, bay leaf and seasonings to pan drippings. Sauté until chicken livers are brown but still slightly pink inside. Discard bay leaf. Add chicken livers several at a time to onions, processing until mixture is smooth. Press through fine sieve. Add remaining butter; mix well. Stir in brandy. Adjust seasonings. Chill well before serving. Yield: 32 servings.

💜 **Approx Per Serving:** Cal 54; Prot 2 g; Carbo 1 g; Fiber <1 g; T Fat 5 g; 80% Calories from Fat; Chol 65 mg; Sod 107 mg.

G. Virginia Murphy, Massachusetts

Krissy's Artichoke Dip

1   15-ounce can artichoke hearts,
    drained
8 ounces cream cheese, softened
1/2 cup mayonnaise
4 ounces mozzarella cheese,
    shredded
1 cup grated Parmesan cheese
1/8 teaspoon garlic powder
1/2 onion, chopped
1/2 cup bread crumbs
Paprika to taste

Chop artichoke hearts coarsely. Combine artichokes and next 6 ingredients in bowl; mix well. Spoon into greased 9-inch baking dish. Sprinkle with bread crumbs and paprika. Bake at 350 degrees for 15 to 20 minutes or until brown. Yield: 6 servings.

♥ **Approx Per Serving:** Cal 440; Prot 15 g; Carbo 13 g; Fiber 1 g;
   T Fat 37 g; 75% Calories from Fat; Chol 78 mg; Sod 777 mg.

Margaret Stepanian, Massachusetts

Fiesta Dip

1 1/2 pounds ground beef
8 ounces cream cheese, softened
1   12-ounce jar picante sauce
12 ounces mozzarella cheese,
    shredded
1   16-ounce package tortilla chips

Brown ground beef in skillet, stirring until crumbly; drain. Layer cream cheese, ground beef, picante sauce and mozzarella cheese in ungreased 9x12-inch baking dish. Bake at 350 degrees for 12 to 15 minutes or until hot and bubbly. Serve with tortilla chips. Yield: 12 servings.

♥ **Approx Per Serving:** Cal 459; Prot 21 g; Carbo 26 g; Fiber 2 g;
   T Fat 31 g; 61% Calories from Fat; Chol 80 mg; Sod 541 mg.

Melanie F. MacDonald, Massachusetts

Taco Dip

This dip is quick and easy and everyone enjoys it.

1   16-ounce can refried beans
1¹/₂ cups sour cream
1   12-ounce jar hot chunky salsa
1 small head lettuce, finely chopped
6 to 8 plum tomatoes, finely
    chopped
1 small onion, chopped
1 small green bell pepper, chopped
8 ounces mozzarella cheese,
    shredded
8 ounces Monterey Jack cheese,
    shredded
2   4-ounce cans sliced black olives
2   16-ounce packages corn chips

Spread beans in greased 9x12-inch baking dish. Bake at 350 degrees for 15 minutes or until warmed through. Layer next 6 ingredients over beans. Mix cheeses together; sprinkle over layers. Top with olives. Serve at room temperature with corn chips. Yield: 100 servings.

♥ **Approx Per Serving:** Cal 84; Prot 2 g; Carbo 7 g; Fiber 1 g;
   T Fat 5 g; 57% Calories from Fat; Chol 5 mg; Sod 155 mg.

Christine M. Brandt, R.N., Massachusetts

Easy Taco Dip

1 envelope taco seasoning mix
8 ounces cream cheese, softened
1¹/₃ cups sour cream
1 cup (or more) chopped tomatoes
1 cup (or more) chopped scallions
1 cup (or more) shredded Cheddar
    cheese

Combine first 3 ingredients in bowl; mix well. Spread in 9-inch serving dish. Layer tomatoes, scallions and cheese over mixture. Serve with chips. Yield: 50 servings.

♥ **Approx Per Serving:** Cal 43; Prot 1 g; Carbo 1 g; Fiber <1 g;
   T Fat 4 g; 76% Calories from Fat; Chol 10 mg; Sod 101 mg.

Rose E. Hines, Massachusetts

Tahitian Meatballs

1½ pounds lean ground beef
⅔ cup crushed butter crackers
⅓ cup finely chopped onion
1 egg, beaten
1½ teaspoons salt
¼ teaspoon ginger
¼ cup milk
2 tablespoons shortening
1   16-ounce can juice-pack
     pineapple
2 tablespoons cornstarch
½ cup packed brown sugar
⅓ cup white vinegar
1 tablespoon soy sauce

Combine ground beef, cracker crumbs, onion, egg, salt, ginger and milk in bowl; mix well. Shape into 1½-inch balls. Fry meatballs several at a time in shortening until brown. Drain on paper towels. Drain pineapple, reserving juice. Combine juice and remaining ingredients in saucepan; mix well. Cook over medium heat for 5 minutes or until thickened, stirring constantly. Stir in pineapple. Add meatballs. Cook until heated through. Pour into serving bowl. Yield: 30 servings.

Approx Per Serving: Cal 96; Prot 5 g; Carbo 9 g; Fiber <1 g;
   T Fat 5 g; 45% Calories from Fat; Chol 22 mg; Sod 178 mg.

Vivian A. Lukas, New Hampshire

Carol's Kielbasa

2   16-ounce jars grape jelly
2   16-ounce packages kielbasa
     sausage
1   16-ounce jar Cheez Whiz

Pour grape jelly into slow cooker. Cut kielbasa sausage into bite-size pieces. Add to jelly, stirring gently. Cook on High for 2 hours or Low for 4 hours. Melt Cheez Whiz in saucepan over low heat. Pour into serving bowl. Serve kielbasa with wooden picks and Cheez Whiz on the side for dipping. May add 1 additional package kielbasa to grape jelly if needed. Yield: 30 servings.

Approx Per Serving: Cal 176; Prot 5 g; Carbo 23 g; Fiber <1 g;
   T Fat 8 g; 38% Calories from Fat; Chol 19 mg; Sod 339 mg.

Carol Maloney, Massachusetts

Marinated Mushrooms

1   16-ounce package mushrooms, cut into bite-sized chunks
1 onion, thinly sliced
2 to 3 tablespoons tarragon
1   8-ounce bottle of Italian salad dressing

*L*ayer mushrooms and onion in shallow bowl. Sprinkle with tarragon; top with Italian salad dressing. Chill, covered, overnight. Drain and serve on lettuce-lined serving plates. Yield: 4 servings.

♥ **Approx Per Serving:** Cal 317; Prot 4 g; Carbo 16 g; Fiber 3 g; T Fat 35 g; 80% Calories from Fat; Chol 0 mg; Sod 285 mg.

Pauline Katz, Massachusetts

Russian Cabbage Pie

2 envelopes yeast
1/2 cup lukewarm water
41/4 cups flour
11/2 teaspoons sugar
1 cup melted margarine
1/2 cup milk, warmed
1   3 to 4-pound head cabbage, chopped
3/4 cup margarine
5 hard-boiled eggs, chopped
1/8 teaspoon baking soda
Salt and pepper to taste
1 egg
1 tablespoon water

*D*issolve yeast in lukewarm water. Combine with 1/4 cup flour and sugar in bowl. Let stand until bubbly. Stir in remaining flour, 1 cup margarine and warm milk. Let stand, covered, in warm place until doubled in bulk. Knead for several minutes on floured surface. Roll into two 11x14-inch rectangles. Line large baking dish with 1 portion. Simmer cabbage in water to cover in saucepan for 4 to 5 minutes. Strain, pressing out liquid. Return to saucepan. Add 3/4 cup margarine. Stir-fry for 4 to 5 minutes or until tender-crisp. Remove from heat. Stir in next 4 ingredients. Pour into prepared dish; cover with remaining dough, sealing edges and cutting vent in center. Brush with mixture of remaining egg and water. Bake at 350 degrees for 35 minutes or until brown. Cool. Cut into squares. Yield: 15 servings.

♥ **Approx Per Serving:** Cal 388; Prot 8 g; Carbo 35 g; Fiber 4 g; T Fat 24 g; 56% Calories from Fat; Chol 86 mg; Sod 308 mg.

Michail and Elena Pankratov, Massachusetts

Pepperoni Pie

4 ounces pepperoni, cut into
   quarters
8 ounces Muenster cheese, cubed
1¹/₂ cups flour
2 cups milk
2 eggs
Oregano to taste

Layer pepperoni and Muenster cheese cubes in greased 9x13-inch baking dish. Combine flour, milk and eggs in bowl; beat well. Pour over layers. Sprinkle with oregano. Bake at 350 degrees for 45 minutes. Cool slightly. Cut into squares. May top with shredded mozzarella cheese. Yield: 15 servings.

♥ **Approx Per Serving:** Cal 169; Prot 8 g; Carbo 12 g; Fiber <1 g;
   T Fat 10 g; 53% Calories from Fat; Chol 50 mg; Sod 272 mg.

Brenda Zielinski, Massachusetts

Greek Spinach Pie

This recipe came from St. Nicholas Greek Orthodox Church in Lexington.

6 10-ounce packages frozen
   chopped spinach, thawed
3 bunches scallions, chopped
¹/₂ bunch parsley, chopped
¹/₂ bunch dill, chopped
3 sprigs of mint, chopped
¹/₄ cup olive oil
12 eggs
8 ounces cottage cheese
1¹/₂ pounds feta cheese, crumbled
White pepper to taste
1 16-ounce package phyllo dough
1¹/₂ cups melted butter

Squeeze spinach in clean towel until dry. Sauté scallions, parsley, dill and mint in olive oil in skillet until scallions are tender. Combine scallion mixture and spinach in bowl; mix well. Cool to room temperature. Beat eggs in mixer bowl. Add cottage cheese, feta cheese and pepper; mix well. Fold in spinach mixture. Layer ³/₅ of the sheets of phyllo dough onto bottom and up sides of greased 12x18-inch baking dish, brushing each with melted butter. Pour in spinach mixture. Layer with remaining phyllo dough, brushing each with butter. Bake at 350 degrees for 1 hour and 15 minutes. Yield: 50 servings.

♥ **Approx Per Serving:** Cal 158; Prot 6 g; Carbo 9 g; Fiber 1 g;
   T Fat 11 g; 62% Calories from Fat; Chol 80 mg; Sod 304 mg.

Judithanne Gray, Massachusetts

Tiropeta

4 eggs
$^1/_8$ teaspoon cinnamon
$^1/_8$ teaspoon nutmeg
8 ounces cream cheese, softened
16 ounces cottage cheese
$^1/_4$ cup chopped parsley
1 pound feta cheese, crumbled
$^1/_4$ teaspoon pepper
12 sheets of phyllo dough
$1^1/_2$ cups melted butter

Beat eggs in mixer bowl until fluffy. Add cinnamon, nutmeg and cream cheese; beat until well blended. Add cottage cheese; mix well. Stir in parsley, feta cheese and pepper. Layer 6 sheets of phyllo dough onto bottom and up sides of buttered 9x13-inch baking dish, brushing each with butter. Pour in cheese mixture. Top with remaining 6 sheets phyllo dough, brushing each with butter and sealing edges. Bake at 350 degrees for 30 to 40 minutes or until golden brown. Cool slightly. Cut into squares. Yield: 12 servings.

♥ **Approx Per Serving:** Cal 505; Prot 17 g; Carbo 17 g; Fiber 1 g; T Fat 42 g; 75% Calories from Fat; Chol 196 mg; Sod 961 mg.

Dimitria P. Chakalis, Massachusetts

Tortellini with Tomato in Garlic Sauce

2   16-ounce packages tortellini
    pasta
4 cups whipping cream
2 chicken bouillon cubes
1 tablespoon minced garlic
$^1/_2$ cup white wine
3 tablespoons butter
3 tablespoons flour
2 tomatoes, chopped
$^1/_2$ cup chopped parsley
$^1/_2$ cup grated Parmesan cheese

Cook tortellini using package directions; drain. Keep warm. Heat cream, bouillon cubes, garlic and white wine in saucepan until hot but not boiling, stirring frequently. Melt butter in skillet. Add flour, stirring until mixed. Cook for 1 minute or until light brown, stirring constantly. Add to hot mixture, stirring until thickened. Stir in tomatoes. Add pasta to tomato sauce, tossing lightly to coat. Serve in individual dishes sprinkled with parsley and Parmesan cheese. Yield: 8 servings.

♥ **Approx Per Serving:** Cal 855; Prot 23 g; Carbo 61 g; Fiber 1 g; T Fat 58 g; 61% Calories from Fat; Chol 233 mg; Sod 887 mg.

John Mills, New Hampshire

Tourtière

1 small onion, chopped
1 teaspoon salt
1/2 teaspoon sage
1 1/2 pounds ground pork and veal
1/4 cup water
1 clove of garlic, minced
3/4 cup mashed potatoes
1 2-crust pie pastry

Combine first 6 ingredients in skillet. Cook for 2 to 5 minutes over medium heat or until meat is light brown, stirring occasionally; drain. Cool slightly. Add mashed potatoes; mix well. Pour into pastry-lined pie plate. Top with remaining pie pastry, sealing edge and cutting vents. Bake at 450 degrees for 15 minutes. Reduce oven temperature to 350 degrees. Bake until brown. Cool slightly. Cut into servings. Yield: 16 servings.

♥ **Approx Per Serving:** Cal 177; Prot 12 g; Carbo 11 g; Fiber 1 g; T Fat 9 g; 47% Calories from Fat; Chol 38 mg; Sod 327 mg.

Frances Mannino, Massachusetts

Tourtière of Quebec

1 pound ground pork
1 small onion, finely chopped
1 small clove of garlic
1/2 teaspoon salt
1/2 teaspoon savory
1/4 teaspoon celery salt or pepper
1/4 teaspoon ground cloves
1/2 cup water
1 2-crust pie pastry

Combine first 8 ingredients in skillet. Cook over medium heat for 20 minutes or until pork is light brown and most of liquid is evaporated, stirring frequently. Remove garlic clove. Spoon into pastry-lined 9-inch pie plate. Top with remaining pie pastry, sealing edge and cutting vents. Bake at 450 degrees for 10 minutes. Reduce oven temperature to 350 degrees. Bake for 20 to 25 minutes longer or until brown. Cool slightly. Cut into servings. Serve with chili sauce or green tomato relish.
Yield: 16 servings.

♥ **Approx Per Serving:** Cal 153; Prot 8 g; Carbo 9 g; Fiber 1 g; T Fat 9 g; 53% Calories from Fat; Chol 21 mg; Sod 244 mg.

Rachel L. Pouliot, Canada

My Own Special Pizza

This is my favorite goody for favorite people.

1   16-ounce package hot roll mix
2 teaspoons vegetable oil
4 ounces mozzarella cheese, shredded
1 pound Italian tomatoes, peeled, ground
2 cloves of garlic, minced
1/8 teaspoon salt
1/8 teaspoon pepper
1/4 teaspoon anise seed
1/4 teaspoon fennel seed
1/4 teaspoon each: basil, oregano, Italian seasoning
3 ounces pepperoni, sliced
1 teaspoon vegetable oil
1   3-ounce can mushrooms, drained

Prepare roll mix using package directions. Oil bowl with 2 teaspoons oil. Place dough in bowl, turning to oil surface. Let stand, covered, until doubled in size. Roll out 2/3 of the dough to fit oiled pizza pan. Layer cheese, tomatoes and garlic on dough. Sprinkle with seasonings. Arrange pepperoni over seasonings. Drizzle with 1 teaspoon oil. Top with mushrooms. Bake at 425 degrees for 20 to 23 minutes or until crust is brown. Cut into servings. May add any favorite toppings before baking. Yield: 14 servings.

♥ **Approx Per Serving:** Cal 206; Prot 7 g; Carbo 27 g; Fiber 1 g;
T Fat 7 g; 33% Calories from Fat; Chol 28 mg; Sod 452 mg.

Ethel O'Connor, Rhode Island

Carolina Pickled Shrimp

1/2 cup canola oil
1/3 cup catsup
2 tablespoons Worcestershire sauce
2 teaspoons sugar
1 teaspoon garlic powder
1/2 teaspoon dry mustard
Hot pepper sauce to taste
1/3 cup white vinegar
1 pound shrimp, cooked
2 small red onions, thinly sliced
2 bay leaves, crushed

Combine first 8 ingredients in bowl; mix well. Layer shrimp, onion slices and bay leaves in shallow bowl. Pour marinade over all. Chill, covered, for 12 hours or longer. Drain and serve with wooden picks. Yield: 10 servings.

♥ **Approx Per Serving:** Cal 162; Prot 8 g; Carbo 7 g; Fiber 1 g;
T Fat 12 g; 63% Calories from Fat; Chol 71 mg; Sod 254 mg.

Olive Milgate, Massachusetts

Shrimp Puffs

1   10-count can refrigerator biscuits
1   6-ounce can tiny shrimp
1/2 cup mayonnaise
1/4 cup grated Parmesan cheese
1/4 cup finely chopped onion
1/2 teaspoon dill
2 teaspoons chopped parsley

*B*ake biscuits using package directions. Combine shrimp and remaining ingredients in bowl; mix well. Split biscuits. Spread mixture on each piece. Place on baking sheet. Broil 3 to 4 minutes or until brown. Serve hot. Yield: 20 servings.

♥ **Approx Per Serving:** Cal 86; Prot 3 g; Carbo 5 g; Fiber <1 g;
   T Fat 6 g; 62% Calories from Fat; Chol 17 mg; Sod 370 mg.

Lauren Hutton, Massachusetts

Spinach Balls

2   10-ounce packages frozen
     chopped spinach, thawed
2 cups herb-seasoned stuffing mix
1/2 cup melted margarine
1/2 cup grated Parmesan cheese
1/2 cup finely shredded Swiss
     cheese
1/2 cup finely shredded Cheddar
     cheese
6 eggs, beaten
1 tablespoon garlic powder
1 teaspoon pepper

*D*rain spinach. Combine spinach and remaining ingredients in bowl; mix well. Let stand for 1 hour. Shape into small balls; place on baking sheet. Bake at 350 degrees for 30 minutes. Serve warm or cold. Yield: 30 servings.

♥ **Approx Per Serving:** Cal 87; Prot 4 g; Carbo 5 g; Fiber 1 g;
   T Fat 6 g; 60% Calories from Fat; Chol 47 mg; Sod 170 mg.

Lola Daigle, Massachusetts

Fried Won Tons

1 cup ground pork
1/4 cup finely chopped water
  chestnuts
1 clove of garlic, minced
1 egg, beaten
1/4 cup finely grated carrot
1/2 cup chopped shrimp
1 scallion, chopped
1 tablespoon soy sauce
1/8 teaspoon pepper
50 won ton wrappers
Oil for deep frying

Combine first 9 ingredients in bowl; mix well. Place 1/2 teaspoon mixture in center of each won ton wrapper. Moisten edges of won ton wrapper; fold up corners, pressing to seal. Deep-fry several at a time in hot oil until golden brown; drain on paper towels. Serve with bottled sweet and sour sauce.
Yield: 50 servings.

Approx Per Serving: Cal 29; Prot 2 g; Carbo 4 g; Fiber <1 g; T Fat 1 g; 17% Calories from Fat; Chol 9 mg; Sod 61 mg. Nutritional analysis does not include oil for deep frying.

Pierre Forgacs, M.D., Massachusetts

Caramel Corn

2 cups packed brown sugar
1/2 cup light corn syrup
1 cup butter
1/4 teaspoon cream of tartar
1 teaspoon salt
1 teaspoon baking soda
6 quarts popped popcorn

Combine first 5 ingredients in saucepan. Bring to a boil. Cook to 260 degrees on candy thermometer, hard-ball stage. Remove from heat. Add baking soda, stirring quickly. Spread popcorn in large baking dish. Pour syrup over popcorn, stirring to coat. Bake at 200 degrees for 1 hour, stirring every 15 minutes. Remove from pan immediately. Cool. Store in tightly covered container.
Yield: 24 servings.

Approx Per Serving: Cal 202; Prot 1 g; Carbo 33 g; Fiber 1 g; T Fat 8 g; 35% Calories from Fat; Chol 21 mg; Sod 201 mg.

Gloria DuPont, Massachusetts

Swedish Nuts

8 ounces blanched almonds
8 ounces walnut halves
2 egg whites
1 cup sugar
1/8 teaspoon salt
1/2 cup butter

Place almonds and walnuts in baking pan. Toast in 325-degree oven until light brown. Beat egg whites until soft peaks form. Add sugar and salt gradually, beating until stiff peaks form. Fold almonds and walnuts into egg whites. Melt butter in 10x15-inch shallow baking pan in 325-degree oven. Spread nut mixture over melted butter. Bake for 30 minutes or until nut coating is brown and no butter remains in pan, stirring every 10 minutes. Cool. Break into serving pieces. Yield: 20 servings.

♥ **Approx Per Serving:** Cal 220; Prot 4 g; Carbo 14 g; Fiber 2 g; T Fat 18 g; 68% Calories from Fat; Chol 12 mg; Sod 60 mg.

Norma E. Bassett, Massachusetts

Swedish Pecans

2 egg whites
1 cup sugar
1/8 teaspoon salt
2 cups pecans
1/2 cup butter

Beat egg whites until soft peaks form. Add sugar and salt gradually, beating until stiff peaks form. Fold pecans into egg whites. Melt butter in 10x10-inch baking pan in 325-degree oven. Spread pecan mixture over melted butter. Bake for 30 minutes or until pecan coating is light brown and no butter remains in pan, stirring every 10 minutes. Yield: 10 servings.

♥ **Approx Per Serving:** Cal 320; Prot 3 g; Carbo 24 g; Fiber 2 g; T Fat 25 g; 68% Calories from Fat; Chol 25 mg; Sod 115 mg.

Ann Foster, Massachusetts

Chinese Fried Walnuts

1 pound walnuts
1/2 to 3/4 cup sugar
1 cup vegetable oil for frying
Salt to taste

Combine walnuts and water to cover in saucepan. Bring to a boil. Boil for 1 minute; drain. Rinse and drain. Place in large bowl. Sprinkle with sugar, stirring to coat. Drop walnuts several at a time in hot oil in skillet. Fry until light brown. Remove with slotted spoon; place on waxed paper. Sprinkle immediately with salt. Yield: 4 servings.

♥ **Approx Per Serving:** Cal 872; Prot 16 g; Carbo 58 g; Fiber 7 g;
T Fat 70 g; 68% Calories from Fat; Chol 0 mg; Sod 12 mg.
Nutritional analysis does not include oil for frying.

Elizabeth Haker, Massachusetts

Frosted Walnuts

1/2 cup sour cream
1 1/2 cups sugar
2 cups walnuts

Combine sour cream and sugar in saucepan; mix well. Bring to a boil. Simmer for 5 minutes, stirring constantly. Pour over walnuts in bowl, stirring to coat walnuts. Spread on greased foil to dry.
Yield: 8 servings.

♥ **Approx Per Serving:** Cal 336; Prot 4 g; Carbo 43 g; Fiber 2 g;
T Fat 19 g; 47% Calories from Fat; Chol 6 mg; Sod 11 mg.

Anne Kennedy, Massachusetts

Mulled Cider

1½ quarts apple cider
¼ cup packed brown sugar
1 cinnamon stick
6 whole cloves
12 allspice berries
Grated rind of 1 orange
Grand Marnier to taste

Combine apple cider, brown sugar and cinnamon stick in slow cooker. Tie cloves, allspice and orange rind in cheesecloth. Add to cider. Cook on High until very hot. Do not boil. Remove spices. Add Grand Marnier to taste.
Yield: 6 servings.

♥ **Approx Per Serving:** Cal 160; Prot <1 g; Carbo 41 g; Fiber <1 g; T Fat <1 g; 2% Calories from Fat; Chol 0 mg; Sod 12 mg.

Patty Brent, Massachusetts

Eggnog

6 egg yolks
¾ cup sugar
6 egg whites
2 cups whipping cream
2 cups milk
½ teaspoon vanilla extract
Nutmeg to taste

Beat egg yolks in mixer until thickened. Add ½ cup sugar; beat well. Beat egg whites in mixer bowl until soft peaks form. Add ¼ cup sugar gradually beating until stiff peaks form. Fold egg yolks, egg whites, cream, milk and vanilla together. Pour into serving cups. Top with nutmeg. Yield: 6 servings.

♥ **Approx Per Serving:** Cal 500; Prot 10 g; Carbo 32 g; Fiber 0 g; T Fat 38 g; 67% Calories from Fat; Chol 333 mg; Sod 122 mg.

Carl Wrubel, Massachusetts

Glögg

1/2 cup golden raisins
1/3 cup sugar
1/4 cup blanched almonds
12 whole cloves
6 cardamom pods
2 cinnamon sticks
11/3 cups water
2 long strips orange rind
3 cups dry red wine
3 cups tawny port wine
11/2 cups cognac

Combine first 6 ingredients in glass container; mix well. Combine mixture, 11/3 cups water and orange rind in heavy enamel or stainless steel saucepan. Bring to a boil. Reduce heat. Simmer for 5 minutes, washing down crystals with brush dipped in cold water. Add red wine and port wine. Bring to a boil over high heat. Remove from heat. Let steep for 2 hours. Bring to a simmer over medium heat. Add cognac. Heat for 1 minute. Strain into hot serving bowl. Ignite. Ladle flaming glögg into heated mugs. Spice mixture may be prepared and stored in airtight plastic wrap until needed. Yield: 12 servings.

Approx Per Serving: Cal 246; Prot 1 g; Carbo 26 g; Fiber 1 g; T Fat 2 g; 6% Calories from Fat; Chol 0 mg; Sod 11 mg.

Sandy Magerer, Massachusetts

Cronin's Mash

Cronin's Mash is a party smash.

2 cups whiskey
1 cup whipping cream
1/4 cup chocolate syrup
1/4 teaspoon coconut extract
1 egg, beaten
1   14-ounce can sweetened
    condensed milk

Combine all ingredients in saucepan; mix well. Heat on low for 2 minutes or until of serving temperature. Serve hot or pour over ice. Yield: 4 servings.

Approx Per Serving: Cal 841; Prot 11 g; Carbo 67 g; Fiber <1 g; T Fat 32 g; 35% Calories from Fat; Chol 168 mg; Sod 181 mg.

Natalie Daddario, Massachusetts

Party Punch

2 6-ounce cans frozen limeade
   concentrate, thawed
1 quart raspberry sherbet
2 quarts ginger ale
¼ bottle of white rum (optional)

Pour thawed limeade into punch bowl. Add sherbet, ginger ale and rum, stirring gently to mix. Mixture will foam. Ladle into serving cups. Yield: 12 servings.

♥ **Approx Per Serving:** Cal 232; Prot 1 g; Carbo 48 g; Fiber <1 g;
   T Fat 1 g; 5% Calories from Fat; Chol 5 mg; Sod 40 mg.

Carol Spencer, Massachusetts

Sparkling Tea Punch

3 quarts ginger ale, chilled
1¼ cups sugar
1 cup hot water
1 cup lemon juice
3 cups orange juice
1 cup pineapple juice
3 cups double-strength tea
1 12-ounce bottle of raspberry
   soda, chilled

Freeze 1 quart ginger ale in ice cube trays. Bring sugar and water to a boil in saucepan. Boil for 5 minutes, stirring constantly. Combine with fruit juices and tea in large container. Chill until serving time. Pour into punch bowl. Add raspberry soda, ginger ale and ginger ale ice cubes. Garnish with mint. Yield: 40 servings.

♥ **Approx Per Serving:** Cal 66; Prot <1 g; Carbo 17 g; Fiber <1 g;
   T Fat <1 g; 1% Calories from Fat; Chol 0 mg; Sod 7 mg.

Lori Hicks, Massachusetts

Hot Toddy

1 teaspoon honey
1 tablespoon lemon juice
3 tablespoons whiskey, rum or brandy
Boiling water
2 whole cloves
1 2-inch strip lemon rind

Combine honey, lemon juice and whiskey in warm mug; mix well. Fill mug with boiling water. Press cloves into lemon rind. Add to hot toddy. Serve immediately. Yield: 1 serving.

♥ **Approx Per Serving:** Cal 121; Prot <1 g; Carbo 7 g; Fiber <1 g;
   T Fat <1 g; 0% Calories from Fat; Chol 0 mg; Sod <1 mg.

Virginia R. Strazzulla, Massachusetts

Soups
&
Salads

Broccoli and Cheese Soup

3/4 cup chopped onion
2 tablespoons butter
6 cups water
6 chicken bouillon cubes
1 teaspoon salt
4 cups uncooked narrow egg
  noodles
2   10-ounce packages frozen
  chopped broccoli
1/8 teaspoon garlic powder
6 cups milk
4 cups shredded Cheddar cheese

Sauté onion in butter in saucepan for 3 minutes. Add water and bouillon cubes. Cook until bouillon dissolves. Add salt. Stir in noodles gradually. Cook for 3 minutes. Stir in broccoli and garlic powder. Cook for 4 minutes or until broccoli is tender. Add milk and cheese. Cook just until cheese melts. Yield: 12 servings.

♥ **Approx Per Serving:** Cal 319; Prot 17 g; Carbo 20 g; Fiber 2 g;
  T Fat 19 g; 54% Calories from Fat; Chol 87 mg; Sod 1068 mg.

Carol Morrell, New Hampshire

Stateside Cheddar Cheese Soup

1/2 cup finely chopped celery
1/2 cup finely chopped leek bulbs
1/2 cup finely chopped carrot
1/4 cup unsalted butter
1/4 cup flour
4 cups beef broth
1   12-ounce bottle of light beer
1 pound Vermont white Cheddar
  cheese, shredded
1 pound New York Cheddar cheese,
  shredded
Salt, cayenne pepper and freshly
  ground black pepper to taste

Sauté celery, leeks and carrot in butter in heavy saucepan over low heat for 3 minutes. Stir in flour. Cook over low heat for 2 minutes. Add beef broth and beer. Simmer for 15 to 20 minutes or until vegetables are tender, stirring occasionally. Add cheeses gradually, whisking until smooth. Season with salt, cayenne pepper and black pepper. Cook just until heated through; do not boil. Garnish with fresh chives.
Yield: 6 servings.

♥ **Approx Per Serving:** Cal 732; Prot 40 g; Carbo 9 g; Fiber 1 g;
  T Fat 58 g; 73% Calories from Fat; Chol 180 mg; Sod 1457 mg.

Bev Marotto, Massachusetts

Cucumber Bisque

4 large cucumbers, peeled, sliced
1 tablespoon grated onion
1/4 cup butter
1 to 3 teaspoons curry powder
1/2 teaspoon salt
2 envelopes instant chicken broth
  mix
1 cup water
1 cup milk
1 cup cream

Sauté cucumbers and onion in butter in large saucepan just until tender. Stir in curry powder. Cook for 2 minutes. Add salt, chicken broth mix and water. Bring to a boil; reduce heat. Simmer for 15 minutes or until cucumber is transparent. Process 1 cup at a time in blender until smooth. Combine with milk and cream in saucepan. Heat just to serving temperature. Garnish servings with chopped chives. Yield: 8 servings.

♥ **Approx Per Serving:** Cal 196; Prot 3 g; Carbo 7 g; Fiber 2 g;
  T Fat 18 g; 81% Calories from Fat; Chol 61 mg; Sod 488 mg.

Gertrude M. Eckert, Massachusetts

Oven Fish Chowder

1 1/4 pounds fish
2 cups chopped potatoes
3/4 cup chopped onion
1/4 cup chopped salt pork
2 cups water
2 to 3 cups milk
Salt and pepper to taste

Cut fish into bite-sized pieces, discarding bones. Process potatoes and onion in food processor fitted with coarse chopping blade. Fry salt pork in 10-quart Dutch oven until brown; remove with slotted spoon. Alternate layers of potato mixture and fish in Dutch oven; top with salt pork. Add water. Bake, covered, at 400 degrees for 15 minutes. Reduce oven temperature to 350 degrees. Bake for 45 minutes longer. Add milk, salt and pepper. Bake just until heated through. Yield: 8 servings.

♥ **Approx Per Serving:** Cal 157; Prot 18 g; Carbo 12 g; Fiber 1 g;
  T Fat 4 g; 23% Calories from Fat; Chol 51 mg; Sod 106 mg.

Judith Avery, Massachusetts

Fisherman's Pot

*This recipe was inspired and adapted from a dish served
in a Gloucester working waterfront restaurant.*

1 28-ounce can whole tomatoes,
    chopped
1 cup chicken broth
1/2 cup thinly sliced celery
1/2 cup sliced onion
1/2 teaspoon finely chopped garlic
1 teaspoon parsley flakes
1 tablespoon sugar
Thyme and pepper to taste
1 teaspoon salt
1 pound fish filets
1/4 cup white wine

Combine tomatoes, chicken broth, celery, onion, garlic, parsley flakes, sugar, thyme, pepper and salt in 3-quart glass dish. Microwave, covered, on High for 5 minutes. Microwave on Medium for 9 to 10 minutes, stirring once. Add fish and wine. Microwave on Medium for 10 minutes or until fish flakes easily, stirring once. Yield: 4 servings.

♥ **Approx Per Serving:** Cal 184; Prot 25 g; Carbo 14 g; Fiber 3 g;
    T Fat 2 g; 12% Calories from Fat; Chol 62 mg; Sod 1159 mg.

Bill Chapin, Massachusetts

Gazpacho

1 medium onion
4 large tomatoes
2 cucumbers
2 green bell peppers
3 cloves of garlic
1 16-ounce can peeled tomatoes
1 cup olive oil
1 cup vinegar
3 slices white bread, torn
Salt to taste

Chop onion, fresh tomatoes, cucumbers, green peppers, garlic and canned tomatoes. Combine in large bowl. Add olive oil, vinegar, bread and salt. Let stand for 2 hours. Process in blender until smooth. Strain into bowl. Add 4 ice cubes; mix well. Chill for 5 hours or longer. Serve in chilled bowls. May top with additional chopped green pepper, cucumber, tomato and onion.
Yield: 8 servings.

♥ **Approx Per Serving:** Cal 316; Prot 3 g; Carbo 17 g; Fiber 3 g;
    T Fat 28 g; 76% Calories from Fat; Chol 0 mg; Sod 154 mg.

Mimi G. Duncan, Florida

Hamburger Stew

1 pound ground beef
1 48-ounce can tomato juice
2 cups sliced carrots
2 cups green beans
2 cups sliced cabbage
1 8-ounce can stewed tomatoes
1 4-ounce can sliced mushrooms
1 medium onion, chopped
2 cups chopped celery
1 tablespoon Worcestershire sauce
1 tablespoon oregano
1 tablespoon basil
1 bay leaf
Salt and pepper to taste

*B*rown ground beef in large sauce-pan, stirring until crumbly; drain. Add tomato juice, carrots, green beans, cabbage, tomatoes, mush-rooms, onion, celery, Worcestershire sauce, oregano, basil, bay leaf, salt and pepper; mix well. Simmer for 2 hours. Discard bay leaf. May add 1 small can minced clams if desired. Yield: 8 servings.

♥ **Approx Per Serving:** Cal 190; Prot 14 g; Carbo 18 g; Fiber 4 g;
T Fat 8 g; 37% Calories from Fat; Chol 37 mg; Sod 854 mg.

Michelle Redmond, R.N., Massachusetts

Mussel Soup

1 12-ounce jar cooked mussels in
   liquid or 12 ounces fresh
   mussels with liquid
1 tablespoon chopped parsley
1 tablespoon celery flakes
2 tablespoons coarsely chopped
   onion
1 cup light cream
3 cups skim milk
1 tablespoon garlic powder
1/8 teaspoon each curry powder,
   oregano and dillweed
1 teaspoon freshly ground pepper

*D*rain mussels, reserving liquid. Cook parsley, celery flakes and onion in reserved mussel liquid in saucepan until tender. Stir in cream, milk, mussels and remaining season-ings. Cook just until heated through; do not boil. Serve with lemon wedges and French bread or New England wafer crackers. Yield: 4 servings.

♥ **Approx Per Serving:** Cal 266; Prot 24 g; Carbo 18 g; Fiber <1 g;
T Fat 10 g; 36% Calories from Fat; Chol 64 mg; Sod 370 mg.

Eloise Houghton, Massachusetts

Lentil Soup

I got this recipe for Shaurabat Adas (Lentil Soup) in Saudi Arabia,
where we lived for 14 years.

1¹/₂ cups dried small red lentils
6 cups water
1 large onion, finely chopped
¹/₄ cup oil
5 cloves of garlic, crushed
2 teaspoons Mixed Spices or
   Baharat
1 29-ounce can tomatoes, crushed
2 limes
Salt and pepper to taste

*B*ring lentils to a boil in 6 cups water in large saucepan, skimming if necessary. Sauté onion in oil in skillet until tender but not brown. Stir in garlic and 2 teaspoons Mixed Spices. Cook for several seconds. Stir in tomatoes. Add to lentils. Pierce limes several times with fork. Add to lentils. Simmer for 40 minutes. Add salt, pepper and additional water if needed for desired consistency. Remove limes. Serve with flat Arabian bread, salad and pickles. Yield: 8 servings.

♥ **Approx Per Serving:** Cal 211; Prot 11 g; Carbo 28 g; Fiber 6 g;
  T Fat 7 g; 30% Calories from Fat; Chol 0 mg; Sod 171 mg.

Mixed Spices or *Baharat*

¹/₂ cup black peppercorns
¹/₄ cup coriander seed
1 cup cassia bark (cinnamon)
¹/₄ cup whole cloves
¹/₃ cup cumin seed
2 teaspoons cardamom seed
4 whole nutmegs
¹/₂ cup paprika

*P*rocess peppercorns, coriander seed, cassia bark, cloves, cumin and cardamom seed in bowl. Process ¹/₂ at a time in blender until finely ground. Combine with nutmegs and paprika in airtight container. Use in soups and recipes based on beef broth or tomatoes. Yield: 2 cups.

♥ Nutritional information for this recipe is not available.

Arlene F. Berg, New York

Parsnip Chowder

¹/₂ cup chopped salt pork
2 cups chopped onions
2 cups chopped peeled parsnips
1 cup chopped peeled potatoes
1 cup canned Italian plum
   tomatoes with liquid
2 cups water
1 cup milk
1 cup light cream
Salt and pepper to taste

Sauté salt pork in large saucepan over medium heat for 10 minutes or until light brown. Remove with slotted spoon and discard. Add onions to drippings in saucepan. Cook until tender and golden brown. Add parsnips, potatoes, undrained tomatoes and water. Cook for 30 minutes or until parsnips are tender. Stir in milk, cream, salt and pepper. Cook until heated through.
Yield: 6 servings.

♥ **Approx Per Serving:** Cal 158; Prot 5 g; Carbo 22 g; Fiber 4 g;
  T Fat 6 g; 35% Calories from Fat; Chol 21 mg; Sod 123 mg.

Grace E. Dare, Massachusetts

Pumpkin Soup

1 pound onions, chopped
2 tablespoons unsalted butter
1 pound ham, chopped
1 pound carrots, finely chopped
2 tomatoes, chopped, seeded
2 10-ounce cans solid-pack
   pumpkin
4 cups chicken stock
2 sprigs of fresh thyme, chopped
2 sprigs of fresh oregano, chopped
1 or 2 bay leaves
Salt and freshly ground pepper to
  taste
2 cups whipping cream

Sauté onions in butter in 2-quart saucepan until tender. Add ham and carrots. Sauté for 5 minutes. Add tomatoes and pumpkin; mix well. Stir in chicken stock, thyme, oregano and bay leaves. Cook just below a simmer for 1 hour. Add salt and pepper. Stir in cream gradually. Cook just until heated through. Discard bay leaves. May make soup in advance, adding cream just before serving.
Yield: 5 servings.

♥ **Approx Per Serving:** Cal 660; Prot 33 g; Carbo 31 g; Fiber 7 g;
  T Fat 47 g; 62% Calories from Fat; Chol 194 mg; Sod 1904 mg.

Allison Stange, Massachusetts

Tomato and Pasta Soup

8 medium tomatoes
1 medium onion, finely chopped
1/4 cup butter
1/3 cup uncooked macaroni
4 cups chicken stock
Saffron to taste
Chili powder and salt to taste

Pour boiling water over tomatoes in bowl, covering completely. Let stand for 1 minute; drain. Add cold water to cover. Let stand for 1 minute; drain. Remove skins; chop. Sauté onion in butter in saucepan until tender. Add pasta. Sauté for 2 minutes. Add tomatoes, chicken stock and saffron. Bring to a boil; reduce heat. Simmer, covered, until pasta is tender. Stir in chili powder and salt. Garnish servings with fresh parsley. Yield: 8 servings.

♥ **Approx Per Serving:** Cal 105; Prot 4 g; Carbo 8 g; Fiber 2 g; T Fat 7 g; 55% Calories from Fat; Chol 16 mg; Sod 447 mg.

Kathleen A. Timony, Massachusetts

Vegetable Chowder

2 cups chopped potatoes
3/4 cup minced onion
1/2 cup chopped celery
1 teaspoon salt
21/2 cups boiling water
1/4 cup flour
1/2 teaspoon dry mustard
11/2 teaspoons salt
1/4 teaspoon pepper
1/4 cup melted butter
2 cups milk
2 cups chopped tomatoes
11/2 teaspoons Worcestershire sauce
1 tablespoon minced parsley
1 cup shredded American cheese

Combine potatoes, onion, celery, 1 teaspoon salt and water in deep saucepan. Simmer for 15 minutes or until vegetables are tender. Blend flour, dry mustard, 11/2 teaspoons salt and pepper into butter in medium saucepan. Cook for several minutes. Stir in milk, tomatoes, Worcestershire sauce and parsley. Cook until thickened, stirring constantly. Stir in cheese until melted. Add to vegetable mixture; mix well. Cook until heated through. May substitute Old English cheese for American cheese. Yield: 6 servings.

♥ **Approx Per Serving:** Cal 272; Prot 10 g; Carbo 22 g; Fiber 2 g; T Fat 17 g; 55% Calories from Fat; Chol 52 mg; Sod 1133 mg.

Eleanor and John Lamont, Massachusetts

Vegetable and Beef Soup

12 ounces beef, cubed
1 tablespoon (or more) olive oil
5 cups water
1½ cups chopped onions
1½ cups chopped celery
1 cup sliced carrots
2 cups chopped zucchini
2 cups finely chopped peeled
   potatoes
1   20-ounce can chick-peas,
   drained, rinsed
1   28-ounce can peeled tomatoes
2 teaspoons basil
1 teaspoon thyme
½ teaspoon pepper

Brown beef in olive oil in saucepan. Add water, onions, celery, carrots, zucchini, potatoes, chick-peas and tomatoes. Stir in basil, thyme and pepper. Simmer until beef and vegetables are tender. Garnish servings with Parmesan cheese. May add beef bouillon if desired.
Yield: 8 servings.

♥ **Approx Per Serving:** Cal 155; Prot 12 g; Carbo 17 g; Fiber 3 g;
   T Fat 5 g; 28% Calories from Fat; Chol 24 mg; Sod 305 mg.

Sandy Duggan, Massachusetts

Five-Way Salad

1   11-ounce can mandarin oranges,
   drained
1   8-ounce can pineapple tidbits,
   drained
1 cup miniature marshmallows
½ cup coconut
1 cup sour cream

Combine mandarin oranges, pineapple, marshmallows and coconut in salad bowl. Add sour cream; mix well. Chill until serving time. Yield: 6 servings.

♥ **Approx Per Serving:** Cal 192; Prot 2 g; Carbo 25 g; Fiber 1 g;
   T Fat 10 g; 45% Calories from Fat; Chol 17 mg; Sod 34 mg.

Ardys M. Proctor, New Hampshire

Pineapple Supreme Salad

1   16-ounce can pineapple slices
1   3-ounce package cherry gelatin
1/2 cup mayonnaise
1/3 cup maraschino cherry juice
8 maraschino cherries

Remove 1 end of pineapple can. Drain juice, leaving pineapple in can. Prepare gelatin according to package directions, using half the amount of water. Pour into pineapple can. Chill until set. Combine mayonnaise and cherry juice in small bowl; mix well. Remove other end of pineapple can. Push gelatin gently from can. Cut into servings between pineapple slices. Place on lettuce-lined salad plates. Top with mayonnaise mixture and cherry. Yield: 8 servings.

💜 **Approx Per Serving:** Cal 174; Prot 1 g; Carbo 19 g; Fiber 1 g; T Fat 11 g; 55% Calories from Fat; Chol 8 mg; Sod 113 mg.

Elizabeth H. Galbraith, New York

Tropical Chicken Salad with Lime Dressing

6 chicken breasts
2 cups water
1 cup white wine
1 teaspoon grated lime rind
1/4 cup lime juice
1 teaspoon crushed dried red pepper
1 teaspoon cumin
1/2 cup vegetable oil
1/4 cup olive oil
1 cup thinly sliced celery
1/2 cup finely chopped green onions
1 cup finely chopped red bell pepper
2 tablespoons minced fresh cilantro
1/2 cup grated coconut
2 bananas, sliced

Rinse chicken well. Combine with water and wine in large skillet. Poach, covered, for 12 to 15 minutes or until cooked through. Drain and cool chicken; cut into 1-inch pieces. Combine next 6 ingredients in bowl; whisk until smooth. Combine chicken with celery, green onions, bell pepper, cilantro and coconut in salad bowl. Add dressing; mix well. Chill until serving time. Add bananas just before serving. Garnish with peanuts, dandelions or lime wedges. Yield: 6 servings.

💜 **Approx Per Serving:** Cal 478; Prot 28 g; Carbo 13 g; Fiber 2 g; T Fat 33 g; 64% Calories from Fat; Chol 72 mg; Sod 86 mg.

Marzina C. Bockler, Massachusetts

Tuna and Pasta Salad

1 16-ounce package ziti or other large pasta
1 8-ounce bottle of light Italian salad dressing
1 12-ounce and 1 6-ounce can tuna, drained, flaked
2 small yellow summer squash, thinly sliced
2 small zucchini, thinly sliced
1 red bell pepper, cut into strips
1/3 cup light mayonnaise
1 large tomato, cut into 8 wedges

Cook pasta using package directions; drain. Add salad dressing to pasta in warm saucepan; mix well. Let stand, covered, for several minutes. Add tuna, yellow squash, zucchini, bell pepper and mayonnaise; mix well. Chill in refrigerator. Spoon onto lettuce-lined salad plates. Top with tomato wedges. Garnish with parsley. Serve with breadsticks and iced tea. Yield: 8 servings.

💜 **Approx Per Serving:** Cal 323; Prot 25 g; Carbo 52 g; Fiber 4 g; T Fat 20 g; 37% Calories from Fat; Chol 35 mg; Sod 396 mg.

Warren Rhodes, Massachusetts

Tortellini-Vegetable Salad

1/2 cup mayonnaise-type salad dressing
1/2 cup grated Parmesan cheese
1/4 cup milk
1 clove of garlic, minced
11/2 teaspoons basil
7 ounces cheese tortellini, cooked
1 cup 11/2-inch zucchini sticks
1 cup 11/2-inch carrot sticks

Combine salad dressing, cheese, milk, garlic and basil in salad bowl; mix well. Add tortellini, zucchini and carrot sticks; mix gently. Chill until serving time. Yield: 6 servings.

💜 **Approx Per Serving:** Cal 225; Prot 9 g; Carbo 23 g; Fiber 1 g; T Fat 11 g; 45% Calories from Fat; Chol 27 mg; Sod 396 mg.

Dayle Caterino, Massachusetts

Broccoli Salad

4 cups broccoli flowerets
1 14-ounce can sweetened
   condensed milk
1 egg
1/2 cup vinegar
3 tablespoons prepared mustard
1/8 teaspoon salt
1/4 cup golden raisins
1/4 cup chopped sweet onion
8 slices bacon, crisp-fried, crumbled

Parboil broccoli just until bright green; drain and cool. Combine condensed milk, egg, vinegar, mustard and salt in blender container; process until smooth and thick. Combine broccoli, raisins, onion and bacon in salad bowl. Add dressing at serving time; mix gently.
Yield: 8 servings.

💜 **Approx Per Serving:** Cal 241; Prot 8 g; Carbo 35 g; Fiber 2 g;
T Fat 9 g; 31% Calories from Fat; Chol 49 mg; Sod 292 mg.

Marion C. Empsall, New York

Three-Bean Salad

1/2 cup vinegar
1/2 cup oil
3/4 cup sugar
1 teaspoon salt
1 teaspoon pepper
1 16-ounce can green beans,
   drained
1 16-ounce can wax beans, drained
1 16-ounce can red kidney beans,
   drained
1/2 cup chopped green bell pepper
1/2 cup chopped red onion

Combine vinegar, oil, sugar, salt and pepper in salad bowl; mix well. Add beans, green pepper and onion; mix well. Chill, covered, overnight. Yield: 10 servings.

💜 **Approx Per Serving:** Cal 214; Prot 4 g; Carbo 27 g; Fiber 5 g;
T Fat 11 g; 45% Calories from Fat; Chol 0 mg; Sod 599 mg.

Karen L. Jackson, Massachusetts

Casabora Salad

*This recipe came from the Casa Restaurant
in Fort Wayne, Indiana.*

1 head iceberg lettuce, torn
1 head romaine lettuce, torn
1 red bell pepper, finely chopped
6 to 10 scallions, chopped
³/₄ cup grated Romano cheese
¹/₂ cup grated Parmesan cheese
1 cup shredded provolone cheese
¹/₂ recipe Casabora Salad Dressing

Combine lettuces, bell pepper and scallions in large salad bowl. Chill until serving time. Add cheeses and Casabora Salad Dressing at serving time; toss to mix well.
Yield: 10 servings.

♥ **Approx Per Serving:** Cal 218; Prot 8 g; Carbo 6 g; Fiber 1 g; T Fat 19 g; 74% Calories from Fat; Chol 18 mg; Sod 344 mg.

Casabora Salad Dressing

¹/₂ cup red wine vinegar
8 ounces olive oil
¹/₄ cup sugar
¹/₄ tube anchovy paste
2 tablespoons cornstarch
³/₄ teaspoon garlic salt
¹/₂ teaspoon oregano
³/₄ teaspoon pepper

Combine vinegar, olive oil, sugar, anchovy paste, cornstarch, garlic salt, oregano and pepper in food processor; process until smooth. Chill until serving time. Yield: 20 servings.

♥ **Approx Per Serving:** Cal 115; Prot <1 g; Carbo 4 g; Fiber <1 g; T Fat 11 g; 87% Calories from Fat; Chol 0 mg; Sod 77 mg.

Elaine Shaunessy, Massachusetts

I had the opportunity to travel to Romania to assist in an orphanage in the town of Brasov. As a pediatric nurse practitioner, I would support and teach the staff on crucial developmental issues.

—Anne Reilly, C.P.N.P.
Lahey Holliston Pediatrics

Marinated Carrots

2 bunches carrots
1 green pepper, chopped
1 onion, chopped
1   10-ounce can tomato soup
1/2 cup vinegar
1/2 cup sugar
1/2 cup oil

Scrape and slice carrots. Bring to a boil in water to cover in saucepan. Cook for 10 to 15 minutes or until tender-crisp; drain. Layer carrots, green pepper and onion in serving dish. Bring soup, vinegar, sugar and oil to a boil in saucepan; stirring frequently. Pour over vegetables. Chill in refrigerator. Yield: 8 servings.

💜 **Approx Per Serving:** Cal 252; Prot 2 g; Carbo 32 g; Fiber 4 g; T Fat 15 g; 49% Calories from Fat; Chol 0 mg; Sod 287 mg.

Dolores Macaulay, Massachusetts

Eggplant Salad

An Armenian recipe commonly included on the meza table.

1 large eggplant
1 large tomato, chopped
1 small onion, finely chopped
1 small green bell pepper, finely
   chopped
1/2 cup finely chopped parsley
1 1/2 teaspoons (about) vinegar
4 teaspoons olive oil
Salt to taste

Place eggplant in 9x13-inch baking dish. Broil until skin is charred on all sides, turning eggplant as 1 side chars. Cool to room temperature. Cut eggplant into halves and scoop pulp into bowl, discarding skin. Mash pulp slightly. Add tomato, onion, green pepper and parsley; mix well. Add vinegar, olive oil and salt; mix well. Chill for 1 1/2 hours. Serve as salad or appetizer. Yield: 8 servings.

💜 **Approx Per Serving:** Cal 42; Prot 1 g; Carbo 5 g; Fiber 2 g; T Fat 2 g; 48% Calories from Fat; Chol 0 mg; Sod 5 mg.

Sarkis and Linda Soukiasian, Massachusetts

Korean Salad

16 ounces fresh spinach, torn
1 cup bean sprouts
3 slices bacon, crisp-fried, crumbled
3 hard-boiled eggs, chopped
1 cup oil
1/4 cup vinegar
1/3 cup catsup
1/2 cup sugar
1 tablespoon Worcestershire sauce
1 onion, grated
Salt to taste

Combine spinach, bean sprouts, bacon and eggs in salad bowl. Combine oil, vinegar, catsup, sugar, Worcestershire sauce, onion and salt in small bowl; mix well. Add to salad at serving time; toss to mix well. Yield: 12 servings.

♥ **Approx Per Serving:** Cal 247; Prot 4 g; Carbo 14 g; Fiber 2 g;
T Fat 21 g; 73% Calories from Fat; Chol 55 mg; Sod 163 mg.

Claire Wilson, M.D., Massachusetts

Mandarin Orange Salad

1/2 teaspoon grated orange rind
1/4 cup fresh orange juice
1/2 cup oil
2 tablespoons sugar
2 tablespoons red wine vinegar
1 tablespoon fresh lemon juice
1/2 tablespoon salt
1 medium head lettuce, chopped
1 small cucumber, thinly sliced
1   11-ounce can mandarin oranges,
    drained
1 avocado, sliced
1/4 cup sliced green onions

Combine orange rind, orange juice, oil, sugar, red wine vinegar, lemon juice and salt in covered jar; shake to mix well. Chill for 24 hours. Combine lettuce, cucumber, mandarin oranges, avocado and green onions in salad bowl. Add dressing; toss gently. Yield: 8 servings.

♥ **Approx Per Serving:** Cal 209; Prot 1 g; Carbo 14 g; Fiber 3 g;
T Fat 18 g; 72% Calories from Fat; Chol 0 mg; Sod 408 mg.

John G. Shaheen, New Hampshire

Mary's Potato Salad

3 pounds potatoes
1 cup (or more) mayonnaise
1/2 medium onion, chopped
2 tablespoons chopped parsley
3 hard-boiled eggs, chopped
Salt to taste
1 tablespoon pepper

Cook potatoes in water in saucepan for 1 hour or until tender; drain. Cool potatoes slightly. Peel and slice potatoes. Combine warm potatoes with mayonnaise in bowl; mix gently. Add onion, parsley, eggs, salt and pepper; mix gently. Serve warm or chilled. Do not substitute salad dressing for mayonnaise. Yield: 8 servings.

💜 **Approx Per Serving:** Cal 379; Prot 6 g; Carbo 36 g; Fiber 3 g; T Fat 24 g; 56% Calories from Fat; Chol 96 mg; Sod 189 mg.

Rick Chevalier, New Hampshire

Raspberry and Walnut Vinaigrette

1 1/2 cups fresh raspberries
1/4 cup water
2 eggs
1 cup olive oil
1/4 cup balsamic vinegar
1/4 cup sugar
Salt to taste
1/2 teaspoon cracked pepper
1/4 cup finely chopped walnuts

Purée raspberries with water in blender. Strain to remove seeds. Combine with eggs and olive oil in blender container. Process at low speed for 20 seconds. Add vinegar, sugar, salt and pepper. Process at low speed for 20 seconds. Fold in walnuts. Store in refrigerator.
Yield: 64 (1-tablespoon) servings.

💜 **Approx Per Serving:** Cal 40; Prot <1 g; Carbo 1 g; Fiber <1 g; T Fat 4 g; 85% Calories from Fat; Chol 7 mg; Sod 2 mg.

James F. Connolly, C.W.C., New Hampshire

Entrées

Beanpot Stew

2½ pounds stew beef
3 or 4 carrots, peeled, cut into
  chunks
1 16-ounce can tomatoes
1 16-ounce green beans, drained
1 onion, thickly sliced
Salt and pepper to taste
3 tablespoons instant tapioca

Combine beef, carrots, tomatoes, green beans, onion, salt and pepper in bowl; mix well. Spoon into 2-quart baking dish. Bake, tightly covered, at 275 degrees for 5½ hours. Stir in tapioca. Bake for 30 minutes longer. Serve with baked potatoes. May cook in slow cooker on High for 6 hours or on Low for 8 hours. Yield: 6 servings.

♥ **Approx Per Serving:** Cal 324; Prot 38 g; Carbo 18 g; Fiber 4 g;
  T Fat 12 g; 31% Calories from Fat; Chol 106 mg; Sod 388 mg.

Joan Donahue, Massachusetts

Beef à la Barbeau

3 pounds stew beef
2 10-ounce cans cream of
  mushroom soup
2 envelopes onion soup mix
1 bay leaf
Paprika to taste
2 soup cans water

Layer beef, mushroom soup and soup mix in baking dish. Add bay leaf and paprika. Pour water over top. Bake, tightly covered, at 350 degrees for 4 hours. Discard bay leaf. Serve beef with cooking juices for gravy. Yield: 8 servings.

♥ **Approx Per Serving:** Cal 315; Prot 33 g; Carbo 8 g; Fiber <1 g;
  T Fat 15 g; 42% Calories from Fat; Chol 99 mg; Sod 1141 mg.

Nancy Barbeau, Massachusetts

Lahey Clinic GLOBAL OUTREACH

Marinated Flank Steak

1 medium onion, sliced
1 clove of garlic, finely chopped
2 tablespoons soy sauce
1/3 cup red wine vinegar
1/2 cup oil
3 sprigs of parsley
1 teaspoon pepper
1   2-pound flank steak

Combine onion, garlic, soy sauce, wine vinegar, oil, parsley and pepper in shallow dish; mix well. Score surface of steak lightly. Add to marinade. Marinate in refrigerator for 2 to 48 hours; drain. Place on rack in broiler pan. Broil close to heat source for 4 minutes on each side. Cut cross grain to serve. Yield: 4 servings.

♥ **Approx Per Serving:** Cal 560; Prot 43 g; Carbo 5 g; Fiber 1 g; T Fat 40 g; 65% Calories from Fat; Chol 128 mg; Sod 585 mg. Nutritional information includes entire amount of marinade.

Barbara Heiss, Massachusetts

Marinated Shish Kabobs

1/2 cup orange juice
2 tablespoons lemon juice
1/4 cup olive oil
2 tablespoons wine vinegar
1/2 cup chopped onion
1 tablespoon Worcestershire sauce
1/4 teaspoon dry mustard
3/4 teaspoon thyme
Salt to taste
1/4 teaspoon pepper
2 pounds boneless beef tip, cubed
12 small white onions
2 small zucchini
2 green bell peppers
6 cherry tomatoes
12 mushrooms

Combine orange juice, lemon juice, olive oil, wine vinegar, onion, Worcestershire sauce, dry mustard, thyme, salt and pepper in bowl; mix well. Add beef. Marinate overnight. Parboil onions; drain. Cut zucchini into 1-inch pieces. Cut each green pepper into 6 pieces. Drain beef, reserving marinade; let beef stand for 1 hour. Thread beef, onions, zucchini, green peppers, tomatoes and mushrooms alternately onto 6 skewers. Broil or grill for 10 minutes, basting with reserved marinade. Serve with rice. Yield: 6 servings.

♥ **Approx Per Serving:** Cal 406; Prot 33 g; Carbo 28 g; Fiber 6 g; T Fat 19 g; 41% Calories from Fat; Chol 85 mg; Sod 81 mg. Nutritional information includes entire amount of marinade.

Helen Freidberg, Massachusetts

Portuguese Roast Beef

1   4 to 5-pound beef roast
1   16-ounce can tomatoes, crushed
1 teaspoon salt
1/2 teaspoon pepper
1 large onion, chopped
3 cloves of garlic, chopped
3/4 cup red wine
1/4 cup red wine vinegar
1 cup water
10 potatoes, peeled

Place roast in roasting pan. Add tomatoes, salt, pepper, onion, garlic, wine, wine vinegar and water in order listed. Roast, covered, at 350 degrees for 1 1/2 hours. Add potatoes. Roast for 1 1/2 hours longer. Serve with pan juices for gravy. Yield: 8 servings.

♥ **Approx Per Serving:** Cal 590; Prot 58 g; Carbo 47 g; Fiber 4 g; T Fat 17 g; 26% Calories from Fat; Chol 159 mg; Sod 457 mg.

Claire M. Simas, Massachusetts

Stuffed Tenderloin of Beef

1   5-pound beef tenderloin, trimmed
1 teaspoon salt
1 teaspoon pepper
2 carrots, coarsely chopped
1 yellow onion, coarsely chopped
1 tablespoon oil
1 clove of garlic, finely chopped
1 1/2 cups finely chopped yellow
    onions
18 pitted black olives, finely chopped
1/2 cup chopped cooked ham
4 ounces mushrooms, finely chopped
1/4 cup finely chopped parsley
2 egg yolks, slightly beaten
2 tablespoons brandy
1/2 cup whole pine nuts
3 tablespoons tawny Port

Slice tenderloin at 3/4-inch intervals, cutting to but not through bottom. Sprinkle with salt and pepper. Sauté carrots and coarsely chopped onion in oil in roasting pan over high heat for 2 minutes. Place beef on top. Combine next 9 ingredients in bowl; mix well. Spoon between slices of beef. Roast at 500 degrees for 5 minutes. Reduce oven temperature to 350 degrees. Roast for 35 minutes longer. Remove to heated platter. Let stand, loosely covered with foil, for 20 minutes. Add wine to roasting pan. Boil on stovetop for 3 minutes. Strain pan juices to serve with beef. Yield: 10 servings.

♥ **Approx Per Serving:** Cal 422; Prot 47 g; Carbo 8 g; Fiber 2 g; T Fat 22 g; 48% Calories from Fat; Chol 174 mg; Sod 453 mg.

David and Mary Shahian, Massachusetts

Polish Stuffed Cabbage

1 pound ground beef
1 cup cooked rice
1 egg
1 small onion, finely chopped
1 teaspoon salt
1 small head cabbage
1   8-ounce can tomato sauce

Mix ground beef, rice, egg, onion and salt in bowl. Add cabbage to boiling water in saucepan. Let stand for several minutes, removing 12 leaves as they loosen. Spoon ground beef mixture onto cabbage leaves. Roll leaves to enclose filling; place in saucepan. Add just enough water to cover. Simmer for 45 minutes. Add tomato sauce. Simmer for 15 minutes longer. Yield: 4 servings.

💜 **Approx Per Serving:** Cal 349; Prot 26 g; Carbo 23 g; Fiber 3 g; T Fat 18 g; 45% Calories from Fat; Chol 127 mg; Sod 971 mg.

Dorothy Dembowski, Massachusetts

Stuffed Cabbage Leaves

1 medium head cabbage
1 pound ground beef
2 cups cooked rice
1/4 cup chopped onion
1 egg, slightly beaten
1 clove of garlic, crushed
1 teaspoon salt
1/4 teaspoon pepper
3 slices bacon, chopped

Remove core from cabbage. Place cabbage cored side down in simmering water in saucepan. Simmer for 10 minutes, turning once. Drain, reserving cooking liquid. Separate 12 cabbage leaves from head. Combine next 7 ingredients in bowl; mix well. Spoon onto cabbage leaves. Fold leaves envelope-style to enclose filling. Sprinkle 1/4 of the bacon in saucepan. Layer cabbage rolls and remaining bacon 1/3 at a time in prepared saucepan. Add 1 cup reserved cooking liquid. Simmer for 40 to 50 minutes or until cooked through. Yield: 4 servings.

💜 **Approx Per Serving:** Cal 409; Prot 27 g; Carbo 30 g; Fiber 2 g; T Fat 20 g; 44% Calories from Fat; Chol 131 mg; Sod 703 mg.

Dolores Pranowski, Massachusetts

Barbara's Mom's Meat Loaf

2 pounds lean ground beef
1 small onion, finely chopped
1/2 cup Italian bread crumbs
2 eggs
1/2 cup low-fat milk
2 teaspoons horseradish
1/2 teaspoon dry mustard
1 teaspoon Worcestershire sauce
3 tablespoons catsup
Salt to taste

Combine ground beef, onion, bread crumbs, eggs, milk, horseradish, dry mustard, Worcestershire sauce, catsup and salt in bowl; mix well. Pack into loaf pan. Bake at 400 degrees on center oven rack for 1 hour and 10 minutes. May add cheese to top or substitute barbecue sauce or salsa for catsup. Yield: 8 servings.

♥ **Approx Per Serving:** Cal 296; Prot 24 g; Carbo 8 g; Fiber 1 g; T Fat 18 g; 56% Calories from Fat; Chol 129 mg; Sod 210 mg.

Sara R. Davies-Lepie, M.D., Massachusetts

Lemon-Barbecued Meat Loaves

1 1/2 pounds lean ground beef
2 cups bread crumbs
1/4 cup lemon juice
1/4 cup minced onion
1 egg
2 1/2 cups barbecue sauce
1 cup packed brown sugar
8 thin lemon slices

Combine ground beef, bread crumbs, lemon juice, onion and egg in bowl; mix well. Shape into 4 individual loaves. Place in greased 9x13-inch baking dish. Bake at 350 degrees for 25 minutes. Combine barbecue sauce and brown sugar in bowl; mix well. Spoon over loaves; top with lemon slices. Bake for 30 minutes longer, basting occasionally.
Yield: 4 servings.

♥ **Approx Per Serving:** Cal 928; Prot 42 g; Carbo 122 g; Fiber 4 g; T Fat 32 g; 30% Calories from Fat; Chol 167 mg; Sod 1787 mg.

Gary and Renee Emmonds, Massachusetts

No-Mess Sloppy Joes

1 pound ground beef
1   15-ounce can Manwich Sloppy
   Joes sauce
2   8-count cans crescent rolls
8 slices American cheese

Brown ground beef in skillet, stirring until crumbly; drain. Add Sloppy Joes sauce; mix well. Separate roll dough into rectangles, pressing perforations to seal. Spoon ground beef mixture onto 1 side of each rectangle; top with 1 slice of cheese. Fold dough over to enclose filling; press edges to seal. Place on baking sheet. Bake using roll can directions. Yield: 8 servings.

♥ **Approx Per Serving:** Cal 451; Prot 21 g; Carbo 29 g; Fiber 0 g; T Fat 28 g; 56% Calories from Fat; Chol 64 mg; Sod 1194 mg.

Terri Palmer, Massachusetts

Quigley's Spaghetti Sauce

1 or 2 cloves of garlic, minced
1 onion, chopped
1 green or red bell pepper, chopped
1 or 2 stalks celery, chopped
1 or 2 tablespoons olive oil
1 pound ground beef
1   28-ounce can tomatoes, crushed
1   8-ounce can tomato sauce
1   6-ounce can tomato paste
1 tablespoon each crushed red
   pepper, oregano, parsley flakes
   and Italian seasoning
1/2 teaspoon each garlic powder,
   onion powder and celery seed
Salt and pepper to taste

Sauté garlic, onion, bell pepper and celery in olive oil in heavy 4 or 5-quart saucepan until onion is tender. Crumble in ground beef. Cook until brown, stirring frequently; drain. Add tomatoes, tomato sauce and tomato paste. Bring to a boil, stirring occasionally. Add seasonings; mix well. Reduce heat. Simmer for 1 hour. Yield: 8 servings.

♥ **Approx Per Serving:** Cal 203; Prot 13 g; Carbo 13 g; Fiber 3 g; T Fat 12 g; 51% Calories from Fat; Chol 37 mg; Sod 388 mg.

Barbara J. Cross, New Hampshire

Ham and Broccoli Casserole

2   10-ounce packages frozen
    broccoli spears
2 cups chopped cooked ham
1   3-ounce can French-fried onions
1 cup shredded Cheddar cheese
1   10-ounce can cream of
    mushroom soup
1/4 cup milk

Microwave broccoli in packages on High for 5 minutes; drain well. Arrange in 8x12-inch glass dish, alternating direction of heads. Top with ham, half the onions and cheese. Pour mixture of soup and milk over top. Microwave, covered, with waxed paper, on High for 8 to 10 minutes. Sprinkle with remaining onions. Microwave, uncovered, for 5 to 6 minutes or until heated through. Yield: 6 servings.

♥ **Approx Per Serving:** Cal 317; Prot 22 g; Carbo 15 g; Fiber 3 g;
   T Fat 19 g; 55% Calories from Fat; Chol 47 mg; Sod 1238 mg.

Sheryl L. Pike, Massachusetts

Ham and Broccoli Quiche

3/4 cup shredded Swiss cheese
3/4 cup shredded Cheddar cheese
1/2 cup chopped cooked ham
1/3 onion, chopped
1 unbaked 9-inch pie shell
1   10-ounce package frozen
    chopped broccoli, cooked
1   12-ounce can evaporated milk
4 eggs, beaten
Salt and pepper to taste

Sprinkle cheeses, ham and onion into pie shell. Spread broccoli over top. Bring evaporated milk to a boil in saucepan. Add to eggs very gradually, stirring constantly. Season with salt and pepper. Spoon over broccoli. Bake at 425 degrees for 15 minutes. Reduce oven temperature to 300 degrees. Bake for 30 minutes longer. Let stand for 10 minutes or longer before serving. Yield: 6 servings.

♥ **Approx Per Serving:** Cal 424; Prot 22 g; Carbo 23 g; Fiber 2 g;
   T Fat 27 g; 58% Calories from Fat; Chol 193 mg; Sod 580 mg.

Veronica Hatfield, New Hampshire

Ham with Shallots

6 shallots, minced
6 tablespoons red wine vinegar
2 tablespoons butter
8 slices boiled ham
1/4 cup Port
2 tablespoons Dijon mustard
2 tablespoons tomato paste
1 cup whipping cream or sour
  cream

Combine shallots with vinegar in saucepan. Simmer until vinegar has evaporated. Add butter. Cook until shallots are tender; remove with slotted spoon. Add ham to saucepan. Sauté for several minutes. Remove to ovenproof serving platter. Add wine to saucepan, stirring to deglaze. Cook until reduced to desired consistency. Add mustard, tomato paste and shallots. Simmer for several minutes. Stir in cream. Cook just until heated through; do not boil. Spoon over ham. Yield: 4 servings.

♥ **Approx Per Serving:** Cal 473; Prot 19 g; Carbo 27 g; Fiber 1 g; T Fat 32 g; 61% Calories from Fat; Chol 128 mg; Sod 1042 mg.

Mrs. Pendennis W. Reed, Massachusetts

Broiled Lamb and Ratatouille

Broiled lamb is a traditional Middle Eastern dish served with Mother's Lebanese pilaf which combines vermicelli browned in butter and rice; garden salad seasoned with mint; and pita bread.

1 small leg of lamb, boned,
  butterflied
1 large eggplant, peeled
2 medium zucchini, sliced
Salt to taste
1 large onion, chopped
1 green bell pepper, slivered
2 cloves of garlic, crushed
1 tablespoon olive oil
4 medium tomatoes, chopped
2 teaspoons Italian seasoning

Grill lamb, covered, over low coals for 1 1/2 hours or until cooked medium. Cut eggplant into 1x1 1/2-inch pieces. Combine with zucchini in bowl; sprinkle lightly with salt. Let stand for 30 minutes. Sauté onion, green pepper and garlic in olive oil in 12-inch skillet. Add eggplant mixture, tomatoes and Italian seasoning. Simmer over low heat for 40 minutes; do not overcook. Serve with lamb. Yield: 6 servings.

♥ **Approx Per Serving:** Cal 221; Prot 24 g; Carbo 12 g; Fiber 5 g; T Fat 9 g; 36% Calories from Fat; Chol 68 mg; Sod 64 mg.

Charles A. Fager, M.D., Massachusetts

Curried Lamb

2 large onions, finely chopped
6 stalks celery, finely chopped
2 small carrots, finely chopped
4 tomatoes, peeled, seeded, finely chopped
2 tablespoons finely chopped parsley
1 cup butter
1/2 cup flour
4 cups hot chicken broth
2 bay leaves
2 cups white wine
Pepper to taste
2 to 4 tablespoons curry powder
1 cup cream
2 pounds lamb, cooked, chopped

Sauté onions, celery, carrots, tomatoes and parsley in butter in saucepan until very tender. Sprinkle with flour; mix well. Add chicken broth and bay leaves. Cook until thickened, stirring constantly. Stir in wine and pepper. Add curry powder and adjust seasonings to taste. Simmer for 30 minutes. Add cream and lamb. Cook until heated through; discard bay leaves. Serve over rice. Garnish with additional chopped parsley. Serve with bowls of chutney, coconut, chopped peanuts, raisins and/or bacon. May substitute shrimp or chicken for lamb. Yield: 8 servings.

♥ **Approx Per Serving:** Cal 588; Prot 26 g; Carbo 18 g; Fiber 4 g; T Fat 42 g; 68% Calories from Fat; Chol 167 mg; Sod 691 mg.

Mrs. James M. Gavin, Florida

Lazy Man's Leg of Lamb

1 cup plain yogurt
1/2 cup chopped fresh mint
3 cloves of garlic, minced
2 tablespoons fresh lemon juice
2 tablespoons Dijon mustard
Salt and pepper to taste
1   7 to 8-pound leg of lamb, boned, butterflied

Combine yogurt, mint, garlic, lemon juice, mustard, salt and pepper in shallow dish; mix well. Trim lamb. Add to marinade. Marinate in refrigerator for 12 to 24 hours; drain. Grill for 5 minutes; turn lamb. Grill for 3 minutes longer for rare. Yield: 12 servings.

♥ **Approx Per Serving:** Cal 365; Prot 51 g; Carbo 2 g; Fiber <1 g; T Fat 16 g; 41% Calories from Fat; Chol 165 mg; Sod 199 mg. Nutritional information includes entire amount of marinade.

Kala Joblon and Stan Mickelson, Massachusetts

Slow and Easy Lamb

1 pound medium onions, sliced
  into 1/4-inch rings
1   41/2 to 5-pound lamb shoulder
1 teaspoon allspice
Salt to taste
1 teaspoon pepper
1 large green bell pepper, sliced
  into 1/4-inch rings
1 large red bell pepper, sliced into
  1/4-inch rings
8 ounces tomatoes, cut into 1/4-inch
  thick slices
1 tablespoon steak sauce
1/2 cup red wine
1/2 cup water
1 pound small potatoes, peeled
1 tablespoon oil
1 lamb stock cube
1 tablespoon flour
1 tablespoon oil

Spread half the onions in heavy 10-inch nonstick saucepan. Place lamb on onions. Sprinkle with allspice, salt and pepper. Top with remaining onions, bell peppers, tomatoes, steak sauce, wine and 1/2 cup water. Simmer, covered, over very low heat for 7 hours; do not lift cover. Peel potatoes and let stand in cold water to cover in saucepan. Add 1 tablespoon oil. Cook for 20 minutes; drain. Place potatoes on baking sheet. Remove lamb from saucepan. Debone lamb and place on warm platter. Stir lamb stock cube into pan juices in saucepan. Blend flour into 1 tablespoon oil in small saucepan. Strain pan juices into flour mixture. Cook until thickened, stirring constantly. Brown potatoes in hot oven. Arrange cooked vegetables and potatoes around lamb. Serve with gravy.
Yield: 7 servings.

♥ **Approx Per Serving:** Cal 689; Prot 72 g; Carbo 22 g; Fiber 3 g;
  T Fat 33 g; 44% Calories from Fat; Chol 238 mg; Sod 279 mg.

Evans Gazala, London

*Twins in Armenia with corneal
scarring and congenital glaucoma*

Devonshire Pork Filets

2 pork filets, cubed
2 ounces brown sugar
2 tablespoons dry mustard
2 tablespoons corn oil
1 onion, chopped
1 apple, chopped
1 envelope white sauce mix
1 cup cider
Juice of 1 orange
Grated orange rind to taste

Coat pork with mixture of brown sugar and dry mustard. Brown in oil in large skillet. Remove to platter. Add onion to skillet. Sauté until tender but not brown. Add apple. Sauté for several minutes; drain skillet. Return pork to skillet. Prepare white sauce mix using package directions, substituting cider for milk. Stir in orange juice and orange rind. Spoon over pork. Simmer for 1½ hours or until tender.
Yield: 2 servings.

Approx Per Serving: Cal 888; Prot 39 g; Carbo 111 g; Fiber 4 g; T Fat 35 g; 34% Calories from Fat; Chol 98 mg; Sod 973 mg.

Ronald W. Owen, Massachusetts

Pork Hawaiian

6 medium pork chops
1   29-ounce can yams, drained
1 large onion, sliced into rings
1   7-ounce can sliced pineapple
3 tablespoons brown mustard
1 cup packed brown sugar

Brown pork chops on both sides in skillet; drain. Place pork chops in 8x11-inch baking pan. Place yams between pork chops. Top with onion rings. Drain pineapple, reserving juice. Combine reserved juice with mustard and brown sugar in bowl; mix well. Spoon over pork chops. Bake at 350 degrees for 45 minutes. Add pineapple slices. Bake for 15 minutes longer. Yield: 6 servings.

Approx Per Serving: Cal 585; Prot 35 g; Carbo 85 g; Fiber 4 g; T Fat 12 g; 18% Calories from Fat; Chol 98 mg; Sod 400 mg.

Sheila A. Shannon, Massachusetts

Scalloped Potatoes and Pork Chops

3¹/₂ pounds potatoes, thinly sliced
1 onion, thinly sliced
1   10-ounce can cream of
   mushroom soup
2 cups milk
4 pork chops

Cook potatoes and onion in water to cover in saucepan for 15 to 20 minutes or until tender; drain. Place vegetables in 3-quart baking dish. Top with mixture of soup and milk. Arrange pork chops over top. Bake at 350 degrees for 30 minutes. Turn pork chops. Bake for 15 minutes longer. Yield: 4 servings.

Approx Per Serving: Cal 731; Prot 44 g; Carbo 93 g; Fiber 7 g; T Fat 20 g; 25% Calories from Fat; Chol 115 mg; Sod 723 mg.

Betty Crogan, Massachusetts

Braised Lemon Veal

1   3-pound rolled leg of veal or
   roast
¹/₄ cup butter
3 tablespoons flour
1 cup water
1 cup dry white wine
3 whole cloves of garlic
1 bay leaf
Salt and pepper to taste
3 egg yolks
Juice of 2 lemons

Brown veal well on all sides in butter in heavy cast-iron pot over high heat. Remove veal from pot. Stir in flour. Cook until brown, stirring constantly. Stir in water gradually. Add wine, garlic, bay leaf, salt and pepper. Cook until thickened, stirring constantly. Return veal to pot. Braise for 1¹/₂ hours; remove from heat. Remove veal to warm serving plate; discard garlic and bay leaf. Whisk in mixture of egg yolks and lemon juice, whisking until thickened; do not heat. Cut veal into serving pieces. Spoon gravy over top. Garnish with parsley. Serve with rice and a green vegetable. Yield: 6 servings.

Approx Per Serving: Cal 392; Prot 47 g; Carbo 5 g; Fiber <1 g; T Fat 17 g; 38% Calories from Fat; Chol 314 mg; Sod 186 mg.

Dorothy McCulloch, Rhode Island

Brisket of Veal Roast

1   3-pound veal brisket
6 ounces chili sauce
3 tablespoons brown sugar
1 cup black coffee

Place veal in baking pan. Add mixture of chili sauce, brown sugar and coffee. Bake, covered, at 350 degrees for 1 hour. Cool and slice veal. Return to baking pan. Bake for 1 to 1 1/2 hours or until tender.
Yield: 8 servings.

♥ **Approx Per Serving:** Cal 223; Prot 34 g; Carbo 10 g; Fiber <1 g; T Fat 5 g; 19% Calories from Fat; Chol 137 mg; Sod 373 mg.

Jeanne Croland, Florida

Baked Hungarian Veal Goulash

4 pounds 1-inch veal cubes
1/4 cup butter
1/4 teaspoon salt
1/8 teaspoon pepper
3   10-ounce cans cream of
    mushroom soup
1/4 cup butter
3 cups sliced onions
1/4 cup water
1/4 teaspoon seasoning salt
1/8 teaspoon Tabasco sauce
1/4 cup sherry
1 cup sour cream
1/8 teaspoon cracked pepper

Brown veal 1/3 at a time in 1/4 cup butter in large skillet, removing to large deep roasting pan. Sprinkle veal with salt and 1/8 teaspoon pepper; spread with soup. Add 1/4 cup butter and onions to skillet. Sauté until golden brown. Spread over veal. Add water, seasoning salt and Tabasco sauce to skillet, stirring to deglaze. Spoon into roasting pan. Bake, covered, at 375 degrees for 45 minutes. Pour wine over top. Bake, uncovered, for 35 minutes. Stir in sour cream; sprinkle with cracked pepper. Mix gently. Bake for 10 minutes longer. Serve over rice.
Yield: 12 servings.

♥ **Approx Per Serving:** Cal 359; Prot 32 g; Carbo 8 g; Fiber 1 g; T Fat 21 g; 54% Calories from Fat; Chol 152 mg; Sod 797 mg.

Eva Litten, Massachusetts

Milanesa de Ternera

This recipe of European origin is a very popular dish in Argentina.

4 6-ounce veal cutlets
Salt and freshly ground pepper to
  taste
1/2 cup flour
1 egg, beaten
1/4 cup water
1 cup bread crumbs
1/4 cup butter

Sprinkle veal with salt and pepper. Coat with flour, shaking off excess. Dip in mixture of egg and water; coat with bread crumbs. Repeat process if desired. Brown on both sides in butter in large skillet. Arrange on warm platter. Garnish with lemon wedges. Serve with mashed potatoes and mixed green salad. Yield: 4 servings.

♥ **Approx Per Serving:** Cal 457; Prot 40 g; Carbo 30 g; Fiber 1 g;
  T Fat 19 g; 38% Calories from Fat; Chol 223 mg; Sod 384 mg.

José A. Gutrecht, M.D., Massachusetts

Spaghetti Pizza

1 16-ounce package uncooked
  spaghetti
2 eggs
1/2 cup skim milk
1/2 teaspoon garlic powder
1 cup shredded skim milk
  mozzarella cheese
1 32-ounce jar spaghetti sauce
2 cups shredded skim milk
  mozzarella cheese
8 ounces pepperoni, sliced

Break spaghetti into 2-inch pieces. Cook using package directions. Drain and cool. Beat eggs in mixer bowl. Add milk, garlic powder and 1 cup cheese; mix well. Add to spaghetti; mix well. Spread evenly in 10x15-inch baking pan. Bake at 400 degrees for 15 minutes. Reduce oven temperature to 350 degrees. Spread spaghetti sauce over spaghetti layer. Top with 2 cups cheese. Arrange pepperoni slices in rows over top. Bake at 350 degrees for 30 minutes. Let stand for 5 minutes before cutting into squares to serve. Yield: 8 servings.

♥ **Approx Per Serving:** Cal 618; Prot 29 g; Carbo 64 g; Fiber 4 g;
  T Fat 27 g; 40% Calories from Fat; Chol 86 mg; Sod 1392 mg.

Sharon E. Alexander, New Hampshire

Two-Crust Pizza

8 ounces bulk Italian sausage
2 recipes pizza dough
1 cup shredded mozzarella cheese
1/2 cup shredded provolone cheese
1 cup pizza sauce
1/2 cup sliced mushrooms
1/2 cup chopped Genoa salami
1 medium onion, sliced
1 cup chopped fresh basil
1 tablespoon olive oil
1 egg, beaten

Cook sausage in skillet, stirring until crumbly; drain. Roll half the pizza dough into 13-inch circle on floured surface. Fit into 10-inch pie plate. Sprinkle with sausage and mixture of cheeses. Top with pizza sauce, mushrooms, salami, onion and basil. Drizzle with olive oil. Roll remaining pizza dough into 11-inch circle on floured surface. Fit over pie. Shape edges into rim, pressing to seal. Prick with fork; brush with egg. Bake at 425 degrees for 30 minutes or until golden. Serve hot or cooled. Yield: 4 servings.

♥ **Approx Per Serving:** Cal 744; Prot 32 g; Carbo 79 g; Fiber 2 g; T Fat 33 g; 40% Calories from Fat; Chol 126 mg; Sod 1827 mg.

Terry Maggiore, Massachusetts

Teen Bean Bake

8 ounces frankfurters
2 16-ounce cans baked beans
1/2 cup catsup
1/2 cup boiling water
1 tablespoon prepared mustard
3/4 cup flour
1 tablespoon sugar
1 1/2 teaspoons baking powder
1 teaspoon salt
2/3 cup cornmeal
1 egg, slightly beaten
2/3 cup milk
3/4 cup melted shortening
1/2 cup finely chopped onion

Cut frankfurters into 1/2-inch pieces. Combine with beans, catsup, boiling water and mustard in bowl; mix well. Spoon into 8x12-inch baking dish. Sift flour, sugar, baking powder and salt into bowl. Stir in cornmeal. Add egg, milk, shortening and onion all at once; mix well. Spoon over casserole. Bake at 400 degrees for 35 to 40 minutes or until golden brown. Serve with a salad and crusty bread to hungry teenagers. Yield: 8 servings.

♥ **Approx Per Serving:** Cal 503; Prot 13 g; Carbo 50 g; Fiber 5 g; T Fat 30 g; 52% Calories from Fat; Chol 44 mg; Sod 1316 mg.

Martha E. Thornton, Florida

Arroz con Pollo

2½ pounds cut-up chicken, skinned
1   14-ounce can chicken broth
⅓ cup water
1   16-ounce can tomatoes
½ cup chopped onion
2 cloves of garlic, minced
¼ teaspoon turmeric
1 bay leaf
½ teaspoon salt
⅛ teaspoon pepper
1 cup uncooked rice
1   10-ounce package frozen peas

Rinse chicken well. Combine with broth, water, tomatoes, onion, garlic, turmeric, bay leaf, salt and pepper in 4½-quart saucepan. Simmer, covered, for 20 minutes. Add rice. Simmer, covered, for 20 minutes. Add peas. Simmer, covered, for 10 minutes longer or until chicken and rice are tender, stirring occasionally. Discard bay leaf. Yield: 5 servings.

♥ **Approx Per Serving:** Cal 430; Prot 41 g; Carbo 43 g; Fiber 5 g; T Fat 10 g; 20% Calories from Fat; Chol 102 mg; Sod 776 mg.

William L. Tanzer, O.D., Massachusetts

Chicken Barbecue

½ cup chopped onion
¼ cup chopped green bell pepper
¼ cup chopped celery
⅓ cup oil
½ cup catsup
¼ cup water
2 tablespoons vinegar
2 tablespoons sugar
1 tablespoon Worcestershire sauce
1 tablespoon prepared mustard
2 teaspoons salt
¼ teaspoon pepper
3 pounds cut-up chicken

Sauté onion, green pepper and celery in oil in skillet until tender but not brown. Add catsup, water, vinegar, sugar, Worcestershire sauce, mustard, salt and pepper; mix well. Simmer over very low heat for 15 minutes. Rinse chicken and pat dry. Arrange in 9x13-inch baking dish. Pour sauce over top. Bake at 400 degrees for 45 to 50 minutes or until cooked through, basting frequently. Serve over sliced cooked potatoes. Yield: 4 servings.

♥ **Approx Per Serving:** Cal 560; Prot 50 g; Carbo 18 g; Fiber 1 g; T Fat 31 g; 51% Calories from Fat; Chol 152 mg; Sod 1661 mg.

Carol Strudas, Massachusetts

Chicken Casserole

2 chickens
1 carrot, chopped
1 stalk celery, chopped
1 onion, chopped
1 bay leaf
Salt and pepper to taste
2 pounds mushrooms, sliced
5 tablespoons butter
2 tablespoons minced onion
2/3 cup butter
3/4 cup flour
4 cups cream
Dry mustard to taste
1 1/2 pounds boiled ham, slivered
8 ounces wild rice, cooked
1/2 cup slivered blanched almonds, toasted

Rinse chickens inside and out. Cook with next 6 ingredients and water to cover in saucepan until tender. Cool in broth. Chop chicken, discarding skin and bones. Skim, strain and reserve 4 cups broth. Sauté mushrooms in 5 tablespoons butter in skillet. Sauté 2 tablespoons onion in 2/3 cup butter in saucepan. Stir in flour until smooth. Add reserved broth and cream gradually. Cook until thickened, stirring constantly. Season with dry mustard, salt and pepper. Add chicken, ham, mushrooms and rice. Spoon into large baking dish. Top with almonds. Bake at 350 degrees for 45 minutes. Yield: 16 servings.

♥ **Approx Per Serving:** Cal 659; Prot 43 g; Carbo 22 g; Fiber 2 g;
T Fat 45 g; 61% Calories from Fat; Chol 212 mg; Sod 956 mg.

Mrs. Robert E. Wise, Florida

Chicken Curry

2/3 cup chopped onion
1 clove of garlic
6 tablespoons butter
6 tablespoons flour
1 teaspoon ground ginger
2 to 3 tablespoons curry powder
1 1/2 teaspoons salt
2 cups milk
1/2 cup coconut milk
1 cup chicken broth
2 cups chopped cooked chicken

Sauté onion and garlic in butter in saucepan until onion is tender; discard garlic. Stir mixture of next 4 ingredients into butter in saucepan. Add milk, coconut milk and broth. Cook over low heat until thickened, stirring constantly; do not boil. Stir in chicken. Cook just until heated through. Serve with chutney, coconut or peanuts. Yield: 6 servings.

♥ **Approx Per Serving:** Cal 322; Prot 18 g; Carbo 14 g; Fiber 2 g;
T Fat 22 g; 61% Calories from Fat; Chol 84 mg; Sod 708 mg.

Lucia Palmer, M.D., Massachusetts

Chicken Fricassee with Meatballs

This recipe came from Vienna by way of my maternal great-grandmother.

1 pound chopped sirloin
1 egg white
2 tablespoons bread crumbs
1/2 cup chopped onion
2 tablespoons water
1 teaspoon oil
1 chicken, cut up
2 tablespoons oil
2 tablespoons tomato paste
1/2 cup chopped onion
3 cups water

Combine chopped sirloin, egg white, bread crumbs, 1/2 cup onion and 2 tablespoons water in bowl; mix well. Shape by soup spoonfuls into meatballs. Brown in 1 teaspoon oil in skillet. Rinse chicken and pat dry. Sauté in 2 tablespoons oil in saucepan; drain. Add tomato paste, 1/2 cup onion, 3 cups water and meatballs; mix gently. Cook, covered, for 20 minutes. Cook, uncovered, for 10 minutes longer or until chicken is cooked through. May substitute whole egg for egg white. Yield: 8 servings.

♥ **Approx Per Serving:** Cal 301; Prot 38 g; Carbo 3 g; Fiber 1 g; T Fat 14 g; 44% Calories from Fat; Chol 109 mg; Sod 122 mg.

Mrs. Morton Zuckerman, New York

Chicken Krahi

This is a classic Pakistani dish.

1 chicken, cut up
Salt and red pepper to taste
2 or 3 tablespoons oil
1 2-inch piece fresh gingerroot, peeled, chopped
3 medium tomatoes, chopped
2 medium hot green peppers, chopped

Rinse chicken and pat dry. Sprinkle with salt and red pepper. Brown in oil in 16-inch skillet until golden brown. Add gingerroot. Sauté for 2 to 3 minutes. Add tomatoes and hot peppers. Sauté for 2 minutes; reduce heat. Simmer until chicken is tender and liquid has evaporated. Yield: 4 servings.

♥ **Approx Per Serving:** Cal 441; Prot 51 g; Carbo 6 g; Fiber 2 g; T Fat 23 g; 48% Calories from Fat; Chol 152 mg; Sod 155 mg.

Aabroo I. Khawaja, Massachusetts

Chicken Marsala

2 pounds cut-up chicken
1 cup bread crumbs
3 tablespoons olive oil
2   8-ounce cans mushrooms,
    drained
1 cup (or more) Marsala

Rinse chicken and pat dry. Coat with bread crumbs. Sauté in olive oil in electric skillet for 10 minutes or until brown on both sides; drain. Place in baking dish. Add mushrooms; pour wine over top. Bake at 300 degrees for 30 minutes or until tender. Yield: 5 servings.

♥ **Approx Per Serving:** Cal 416; Prot 31 g; Carbo 25 g; Fiber 3 g;
   T Fat 16 g; 35% Calories from Fat; Chol 82 mg; Sod 615 mg.

Mrs. Peter Volpe, Massachusetts

Chicken Parmigiana

²/₃ cup instant potato flakes
2 tablespoons grated Parmesan
   cheese
1 teaspoon salt
¹/₄ teaspoon pepper
1 egg
2 tablespoons water
1   2¹/₂ to 3-pound chicken, cut up
3 tablespoons melted margarine
6 to 8 ounces uncooked spaghetti
¹/₄ cup grated Parmesan cheese
3 tablespoons margarine
1   16-ounce can stewed tomatoes
¹/₂ teaspoon oregano

Mix potato flakes, 2 tablespoons cheese, salt and pepper in large plastic bag. Beat egg with water in shallow dish. Rinse chicken and pat dry. Dip in egg mixture; coat with potato flake mixture. Arrange skin side up in ungreased 8x12-inch baking dish. Drizzle with 3 tablespoons melted margarine. Bake at 375 degrees for 50 to 60 minutes or until golden brown and tender. Cook spaghetti using package directions; drain and rinse with hot water. Toss with ¹/₄ cup cheese and 3 tablespoons margarine in saucepan; keep warm. Simmer tomatoes and oregano in saucepan until heated through. Spoon spaghetti onto serving platter. Top with chicken and tomatoes. Yield: 4 servings.

♥ **Approx Per Serving:** Cal 895; Prot 65 g; Carbo 80 g; Fiber 4 g;
   T Fat 34 g; 35% Calories from Fat; Chol 211 mg; Sod 1450 mg.

Florence L. Brackett, Massachusetts

Chicken Waikiki Beach

1 chicken, cut into quarters
1/2 cup flour
1/3 cup oil
1 teaspoon salt
1/4 teaspoon pepper
1 20-ounce can sliced pineapple
1 cup sugar
2 tablespoons cornstarch
3/4 cup cider vinegar
1 tablespoon soy sauce
1/4 teaspoon ginger
1 chicken bouillon cube
1 large green bell pepper, sliced
  into 1/4-inch rings

Rinse chicken and pat dry. Coat with flour. Brown in oil in skillet. Place skin side up in shallow baking pan. Sprinkle with salt and pepper. Drain pineapple, reserving syrup. Add enough water to reserved syrup to measure 1 1/4 cups. Mix with next 6 ingredients in saucepan. Bring to a boil, stirring constantly. Cook for 2 minutes, stirring constantly. Pour over chicken. Bake at 350 degrees for 30 minutes. Add pineapple and green pepper. Bake for 30 minutes or until chicken is tender. Yield: 4 servings.

Approx Per Serving: Cal 877; Prot 52 g; Carbo 99 g; Fiber 2 g; T Fat 31 g; 32% Calories from Fat; Chol 152 mg; Sod 1229 mg.

Rona P. DiPietro, Massachusetts

Coq au Vin

1 2 1/2-pound chicken, quartered
2 to 3 tablespoons margarine
1 tablespoon olive oil
8 small white onions
8 small whole mushrooms
2/3 cup sliced green onions
1 clove of garlic, sliced
2 tablespoons flour
1/4 teaspoon thyme
1 teaspoon salt
1/8 teaspoon pepper
2 cups Burgundy
1 cup canned chicken broth
8 each small new potatoes and carrots

Rinse chicken and pat dry. Brown in margarine and olive oil in Dutch oven; remove chicken. Add next 4 vegetables. Cook, covered, for 10 minutes, stirring occasionally; remove from heat. Stir in flour, thyme, salt and pepper. Add wine and chicken broth gradually. Bring to a boil, stirring constantly. Add potatoes, carrots and chicken; mix gently. Bake at 400 degrees for 1 hour and 50 minutes or until chicken and potatoes are tender. Yield: 4 servings.

Approx Per Serving: Cal 731; Prot 50 g; Carbo 52 g; Fiber 10 g; T Fat 30 g; 37% Calories from Fat; Chol 127 mg; Sod 1910 mg.

Pamela Gossman, Massachusetts

Country-Style Chicken

1 3¹/₂-pound chicken, cut up
2 tablespoons flour
Salt and pepper to taste
3 tablespoons oil
12 small white onions
3 stalks celery, chopped
4 to 6 carrots, cut into 2 to 4-inch
    pieces
2 tomatoes, cut into quarters
6 potatoes
¹/₂ green bell pepper, chopped
12 mushrooms
1 bay leaf
¹/₄ teaspoon rosemary
¹/₂ teaspoon thyme
1 chicken bouillon cube
1 cup hot water

Rinse chicken and pat dry; trim fat. Coat with mixture of flour, salt and pepper. Sauté in oil in skillet over medium heat; remove to baking pan. Add onions, celery and carrots to drippings in skillet. Sauté for several minutes. Spoon over chicken. Add tomatoes, potatoes, green pepper, mushrooms, bay leaf, rosemary, thyme, salt and pepper to chicken. Dissolve bouillon in hot water. Pour over top. Bake at 350 degrees until chicken is tender, basting occasionally. Discard bay leaf. Serve with green salad. Yield: 6 servings.

♥ **Approx Per Serving:** Cal 572; Prot 46 g; Carbo 59 g; Fiber 10 g;
    T Fat 18 g; 28% Calories from Fat; Chol 118 mg; Sod 365 mg.

Lucie-Anne Cormier, Canada

Stuffed Chicken with Zucchini

1 pound zucchini, shredded
3 tablespoons butter
3 slices white bread, crumbled
1 egg
¹/₄ cup grated Parmesan cheese
¹/₈ teaspoon each salt and pepper
2 chickens, cut into quarters

Sauté zucchini in butter in saucepan over medium heat for 2 minutes or until tender; remove from heat. Add bread crumbs, egg, cheese, salt and pepper. Rinse chicken and pat dry. Loosen skin carefully from chicken to form pockets. Spoon zucchini mixture into pockets. Arrange in 9x13-inch baking dish. Bake at 400 degrees for 50 minutes. Yield: 8 servings.

♥ **Approx Per Serving:** Cal 419; Prot 53 g; Carbo 7 g; Fiber 1 g;
    T Fat 19 g; 42% Calories from Fat; Chol 192 mg; Sod 326 mg.

Diane Marasca, Massachusetts

Vindaloo

2 teaspoons cumin seed
2 or 3 dried hot chili peppers
1 teaspoon black peppercorns
1 teaspoon cardamom
1   3-inch cinnamon stick
1 teaspoon fenugreek seed
5 tablespoons wine vinegar
1¹/₂ teaspoons salt
1 large clove of garlic
1   1-inch piece of gingerroot,
   scraped
2 to 3 tablespoons water
1 tablespoon coriander seed
¹/₂ teaspoon turmeric
1 tablespoon oil
1 pound boned chicken, skinned
2 pounds pork, cubed
2 tablespoons oil
2 to 3 tablespoons water

Combine first 6 ingredients in spice mill; grind until smooth. Mix with vinegar and salt in small bowl. Process garlic and ginger with 2 to 3 tablespoons water in blender or food processor to form paste. Sauté garlic paste, coriander, turmeric and ground spices in 1 tablespoon oil in large saucepan; set aside. Rinse chicken and pat dry. Cut into bite-sized pieces. Brown chicken and pork in 2 tablespoons oil in skillet. Add to saucepan with enough remaining water to make sauce of desired consistency. Simmer until chicken and pork are tender, stirring occasionally and adding additional water as needed. Yield: 6 servings.

♥ **Approx Per Serving:** Cal 365; Prot 42 g; Carbo 4 g; Fiber <1 g;
   T Fat 20 g; 49% Calories from Fat; Chol 126 mg; Sod 641 mg.

Fern Meyers, Massachusetts

Cheddar Chicken

2 cups butter cracker crumbs
1 cup shredded Cheddar cheese
1¹/₂ tablespoons parsley
1¹/₂ teaspoons minced garlic
6 chicken breast filets
¹/₄ cup melted butter, cooled

Mix cracker crumbs, cheese, parsley and garlic in bowl. Rinse chicken and pat dry. Dip into butter; coat with crumb mixture, pressing crumbs onto chicken. Arrange in baking dish. Bake at 350 degrees for 35 minutes or until chicken is cooked through. Yield: 6 servings.

♥ **Approx Per Serving:** Cal 426; Prot 33 g; Carbo 21 g; Fiber <1 g;
   T Fat 26 g; 52% Calories from Fat; Chol 113 mg; Sod 525 mg.

Maribeth Leahy, Massachusetts

Chicken Chablis

4 chicken breast filets
Nutmeg and salt to taste
3 tablespoons butter
3 tablespoons minced onion
8 ounces fresh mushrooms, cut into
  quarters
1 red and 1 green bell pepper, cut
  into 1/4-inch slices
3 cloves of garlic, minced
2/3 cup Chablis
1 teaspoon cornstarch
1/4 cup water

Rinse chicken and pat dry. Sprinkle both sides with nutmeg and salt. Brown in butter in skillet. Add onion, mushrooms, bell peppers, garlic and wine. Bring to a boil; reduce heat. Simmer, covered, for 20 minutes. Remove chicken to warm platter. Cook pan juices until slightly reduced. Stir in mixture of cornstarch and water. Cook until thickened, stirring constantly. Spoon over chicken. Serve with rice pilaf and a green vegetable. Yield: 4 servings.

♥ **Approx Per Serving:** Cal 274; Prot 28 g; Carbo 7 g; Fiber 2 g;
  T Fat 12 g; 39% Calories from Fat; Chol 96 mg; Sod 141 mg.

Chris and Carol Kuhn, Massachusetts

Chicken Delicious

6 chicken breasts, skinned
1 10-ounce can cream of
   mushroom soup
1 10-ounce can cream of chicken
   soup
1 cup sour cream
1/2 cup slivered almonds

Rinse chicken and pat dry. Arrange in 6x12-inch baking dish. Spread with soups and sour cream; sprinkle with almonds. Bake, covered, with foil, at 350 degrees for 1 hour. Bake, uncovered, for 30 minutes longer. Yield: 6 servings.

♥ **Approx Per Serving:** Cal 381; Prot 32 g; Carbo 11 g; Fiber 1 g;
  T Fat 23 g; 55% Calories from Fat; Chol 94 mg; Sod 839 mg.

Sara K. Robinson, Massachusetts

Chicken Italiano

2 chicken breast filets
1 cup sliced mushrooms
1/3 cup light Italian salad dressing
1 clove of garlic, minced
1 large onion, chopped
1 tablespoon olive oil
2 small zucchini, cut into halves
   lengthwise, sliced
2 large tomatoes, chopped
3/4 cup chicken broth
8 ounces sliced part skim-milk
   mozzarella cheese

Rinse chicken and pat dry; cut into bite-sized pieces. Combine with mushrooms and salad dressing in bowl. Chill for 1 hour. Sauté garlic and onion in olive oil in large skillet. Add chicken mixture to skillet. Cook until light brown. Remove chicken and vegetables. Add zucchini to drippings in skillet. Sauté until tender. Return chicken and vegetables to skillet. Add tomatoes and chicken broth; reduce heat. Top with cheese. Simmer, covered, until cheese melts. Serve over pasta. Yield: 4 servings.

♥ **Approx Per Serving:** Cal 300; Prot 30 g; Carbo 11 g; Fiber 2 g;
   T Fat 16 g; 46% Calories from Fat; Chol 69 mg; Sod 606 mg.

Hillary Wright, R.D., Massachusetts

Chicken Loaf

10 large mushrooms, sliced
1 teaspoon onion powder
1 3/4 pounds ground chicken breast
1/2 teaspoon garlic powder
Low-sodium salt substitute to taste
1/2 cup (about) cornflake crumbs
1/3 cup (about) canned chicken
   broth
1/4 cup (about) light catsup

Sprinkle mushrooms with half the onion powder in colander; let stand for several minutes. Combine chicken with remaining seasonings in bowl; mix well. Add half the cornflake crumbs and enough broth to make of light but not thin consistency, mixing well. Spread a thin layer of chicken in glass loaf pan. Layer with half the catsup, mushrooms, remaining chicken, catsup and cornflake crumbs. Bake at 325 degrees for 1 hour. Yield: 4 servings.

♥ **Approx Per Serving:** Cal 301; Prot 49 g; Carbo 12 g; Fiber 1 g;
   T Fat 6 g; 17% Calories from Fat; Chol 126 mg; Sod 392 mg.

Leatrice Chafetz, Massachusetts

Chicken and Rice

This quick meal is typically served in Japanese homes and neighborhood restaurants.

1¹/₃ cups 1-inch chicken cubes
2 tablespoons sake
¹/₃ cup minced onion
2 tablespoons oil
6 cups cooked medium-grain rice
1 cup catsup
¹/₂ teaspoon salt
¹/₄ teaspoon pepper
¹/₄ cup frozen green peas

Rinse chicken and pat dry. Combine with sake in bowl. Marinate in refrigerator for 15 to 30 minutes. Stir-fry onion in oil in wok or heavy skillet until tender. Add chicken. Stir-fry over medium-high heat for 10 minutes. Mix in rice; push chicken and rice to 1 side of wok. Add catsup to other side of wok. Cook for 2 minutes. Stir into chicken mixture; season with salt and pepper. Add peas. Serve immediately.
Yield: 4 cups.

♥ **Approx Per Serving:** Cal 572; Prot 22 g; Carbo 94 g; Fiber 3 g; T Fat 11 g; 18% Calories from Fat; Chol 42 mg; Sod 1028 mg.

John and Kazuko Beamis, Massachusetts

Chix Phillipé

1 6-ounce chicken breast filet
1 tablespoon flour
Salt and pepper to taste
1 tablespoon olive oil
1 clove of garlic, minced
3 jumbo green olives, sliced
1 tablespoon capers
2 ounces white wine
1 teaspoon finely chopped parsley
1 6-ounce can tomatoes, chopped

Rinse chicken and pat dry. Coat with flour, salt and pepper. Sauté in olive oil in medium sauté pan. Remove chicken. Add garlic, olives and capers to drippings in sauté pan. Sauté for several minutes. Add wine. Cook until liquid is reduced by ¹/₂. Stir in parsley and tomatoes. Simmer for 3 minutes. Add chicken. Simmer just until heated through. Serve with pasta and Italian-style broccoli.
Yield: 1 serving.

♥ **Approx Per Serving:** Cal 448; Prot 42 g; Carbo 15 g; Fiber 3 g; T Fat 20 g; 41% Calories from Fat; Chol 108 mg; Sod 656 mg.

Mark P. Roche, Massachusetts

Chicken and Rice Casserole Supreme

1 cup uncooked rice
1 envelope onion soup mix
8 chicken breasts
1   10-ounce can cream of
   mushroom soup
1 cup boiling water
1 cup white wine
1   3-ounce can French-fried onions

Spread rice evenly in greased 9x13-inch baking pan. Sprinkle with soup mix. Rinse chicken and pat dry. Arrange over rice; spread with mushroom soup. Add water and wine around edges of pan. Bake, covered with foil, at 350 degrees for 1½ hours. Sprinkle with onions. Bake, uncovered, for 20 minutes longer. Yield: 8 servings.

💜 **Approx Per Serving:** Cal 348; Prot 30 g; Carbo 26 g; Fiber <1 g; T Fat 11 g; 28% Calories from Fat; Chol 73 mg; Sod 500 mg.

Sylvia Izen, Massachusetts

Chicken-Spaghetti Casserole

8 ounces fresh or canned
   mushrooms
1 small onion, chopped
¼ cup margarine
12 ounces spaghetti, cooked
3½ cups chopped cooked chicken
⅓ green bell pepper, chopped
1 cup sliced stuffed olives
1   8-ounce can tomato sauce
1 teaspoon (scant) salt
1 cup shredded sharp Cheddar
   cheese

Sauté mushrooms and onion in margarine in saucepan for 5 minutes. Add spaghetti, chicken, green pepper, olives, tomato sauce and salt; mix well. Spoon into greased baking dish. Top with cheese. Bake at 350 degrees for 45 minutes. May substitute black olives for stuffed olives. Yield: 8 servings.

💜 **Approx Per Serving:** Cal 427; Prot 28 g; Carbo 37 g; Fiber 4 g; T Fat 19 g; 40% Calories from Fat; Chol 70 mg; Sod 1158 mg.

Alyshia Gibbs, New Hampshire

Chicken Verdeccio

1   16-ounce can artichoke hearts
4 chicken breast filets
1/2 cup flour
1/2 cup butter
1 tablespoon oil
4 cups sliced fresh mushrooms
4 cloves of garlic, minced
Juice of 1 lemon
1 to 1 1/2 cups sherry

Drain artichoke hearts, reserving liquid. Cut chicken into bite-sized pieces; rinse and pat dry. Coat with flour. Cook in butter and oil in large cast-iron skillet for 10 minutes or until light brown. Add mushrooms, garlic, artichoke hearts, lemon juice and wine; mix well. Simmer until chicken is cooked through and mixture is smooth, stirring occasionally and adding some of the reserved artichoke liquid if needed for desired consistency. Serve with rice pilaf and tossed salad. Yield: 4 servings.

♥ **Approx Per Serving:** Cal 599; Prot 31 g; Carbo 22 g; Fiber 1 g;
T Fat 31 g; 47% Calories from Fat; Chol 134 mg; Sod 550 mg.

Susan S. Frary, Massachusetts

Judy's Cranberry Chicken

1   16-ounce can whole cranberry
    sauce
1 envelope onion soup mix
1   8-ounce bottle of light Catalina
    salad dressing
2 tablespoons apricot sauce
10 chicken breast filets

Combine cranberry sauce, soup mix, salad dressing and apricot sauce in bowl; mix well. Spread in 9x13-inch baking dish. Rinse chicken and pat dry. Arrange in prepared dish. Bake at 325 degrees for 1 hour or until tender. Serve over rice. Yield: 10 servings.

♥ **Approx Per Serving:** Cal 268; Prot 27 g; Carbo 25 g; Fiber 1 g;
T Fat 6 g; 22% Calories from Fat; Chol 72 mg; Sod 414 mg.
Nutritional information does not include apricot sauce.

Ellen Fishman, Massachusetts

Crab-Stuffed Chicken Breasts

6 chicken breast filets
Salt and pepper to taste
1 medium onion, chopped
2 stalks celery, chopped
3 tablespoons butter
3 tablespoons dry white wine
1 6-ounce can crab meat, rinsed,
   drained
1/2 cup herb-seasoned stuffing mix
1/4 cup flour
1/2 teaspoon paprika
2 tablespoons melted butter
1 11/4-ounce envelope Hollandaise
   sauce mix
3/4 cup milk
2 tablespoons dry white wine
1/2 cup shredded Swiss cheese

Rinse chicken and pat dry; sprinkle with salt and pepper. Sauté onion and celery in 3 tablespoons butter in skillet until tender; remove from heat. Stir in 3 tablespoons wine, crab meat and stuffing mix. Spoon onto chicken. Roll chicken to enclose filling; secure with wooden picks. Coat with mixture of flour and paprika. Arrange in 9x13-inch baking dish; drizzle with 2 tablespoons melted butter. Bake at 375 degrees for 1 hour. Place on serving platter; discard wooden picks. Blend Hollandaise sauce mix and milk in saucepan. Cook until thickened, stirring constantly. Stir in 2 tablespoons wine and cheese. Cook just until cheese melts. Serve with chicken rolls. Yield: 6 servings.

♥ **Approx Per Serving:** Cal 364; Prot 38 g; Carbo 12 g; Fiber 1 g;
T Fat 17 g; 43% Calories from Fat; Chol 136 mg; Sod 366 mg.
Nutritional information does not include Hollandaise sauce mix.

Arlene Coughlin, Massachusetts

Drunken Chicken

4 chicken breast filets
1/2 cup red wine
1/2 cup catsup
1/2 cup packed brown sugar

Rinse chicken and pat dry. Arrange in 9x13-inch baking dish. Combine wine, catsup and brown sugar in bowl; mix well. Spoon over chicken. Bake at 325 degrees for 1 hour, basting frequently. May substitute white wine for red wine. Yield: 4 servings.

♥ **Approx Per Serving:** Cal 326; Prot 27 g; Carbo 42 g; Fiber 1 g;
T Fat 3 g; 9% Calories from Fat; Chol 72 mg; Sod 436 mg.

Margaret M. Hurley, Massachusetts

Sesame Chicken

1 large chicken breast
12 ounces uncooked angel hair pasta or vermicelli
4 teaspoons sesame oil
1/4 cup tahini paste
3 tablespoons water
3 tablespoons reduced-sodium soy sauce
2 tablespoons red wine vinegar
1/4 cup peanut oil
2 tablespoons chopped garlic
1/4 teaspoon chili oil

Rinse chicken well. Cook in water to cover in saucepan until tender. Drain, reserving broth. Shred chicken. Cook pasta *al dente* in reserved broth in saucepan; drain and rinse in cold water. Combine pasta, sesame oil and chicken in bowl. Combine tahini paste, water, soy sauce, wine vinegar, oil, garlic and chili oil in bowl; mix well. Add to chicken mixture; mix well. Serve at room temperature. May substitute corn oil for peanut oil. Yield: 4 servings.

💜 **Approx Per Serving:** Cal 620; Prot 20 g; Carbo 70 g; Fiber 2 g; T Fat 29 g; 42% Calories from Fat; Chol 18 mg; Sod 315 mg.

Susan S. Foley, Massachusetts

Teriyaki Chicken

3 tablespoons olive oil
1/2 cup reduced-sodium soy sauce
1/4 cup orange juice
1/2 teaspoon ginger
1 medium onion, chopped
1 tablespoon olive oil
4 chicken breast filets

Combine 3 tablespoons olive oil, soy sauce, orange juice and ginger in bowl; mix well. Cut chicken into small pieces; rinse and pat dry. Add to marinade; mix well. Marinate in refrigerator for 1 hour or longer. Stir-fry onion in 1 tablespoon olive oil in medium skillet. Add chicken and marinade. Stir-fry for 5 to 10 minutes or until chicken is cooked through. Serve over rice. Yield: 4 servings.

💜 **Approx Per Serving:** Cal 292; Prot 27 g; Carbo 8 g; Fiber 1 g; T Fat 17 g; 52% Calories from Fat; Chol 72 mg; Sod 844 mg.

Mary V. Dunmore, Massachusetts

Sancocho from the Dominican Republic

2 chickens or 1   4-pound hen
2 pounds pork chops
1 pound bacon
1½ pounds goat
1 bar longaniza (long sausage)
4 green platanos (plantain)
2 pounds yuca (tapioca)
2 pounds squash
2 pounds sweet potatoes
5 corn on the cobs
2 pounds ñame (yam)
6 liters waters
1½ teaspoons oregano

5 tablespoons salt
2 tablespoons sour orange juice
2 green peppers, cut in fourths
5 small green peppers, cut in half
1 medium onion, grated
1 tablespoon garlic, mashed
1 bay leaf
1 leaf cilantrico (coriander)
1 leaf puerro (leek)
2 leaves cilantro ancho (large leek)
1 chicken and 1 beef cube
2 tablespoons vinagre (vinegar)

From the day before in order to save time, you can prepare your meat in the following way. Cut your chicken in pieces and wash with sour orange juice, this process takes away the excess grease, season the meat with peppers, onion, garlic, English sauce (optional) sliced tomatoes, bay leaf and salt. Leave set 30 minutes. Start cooking the chicken without adding tomatoes, and trying to stay with a lot of sauce. Just cook enough until tender. Prepare pork chops and goat the same way as you prepare the chicken, but not together with a lot of sauce. Reserve. Do not season the bacon, because bacon has its own flavor. Cut bacon in pieces and cook in a small amount of water; do not let it get too soft. Cut the longaniza (long sausage) in pieces not too small, and fry in a little bit of oil. Keep it with the oil. Cut all remaining vegetables in pieces, put in water with salt, for them not to discolor. Leave aside until time when you need to add to the other ingredients. In a very large pot (or in 2 smaller pots) boil the 6 liters of water with salt, add onion, spice peppers, bay leaf, squash, corn platanos (plantain) and yautia. When half way done add remaining veggies. Pour through a colander the sauce with the meats, except the longaniza (long sausage) and oregano. Add the 2 tablespoons of oil from the fried longaniza (long sausage) plus the sour orange juice, vinegar and garlic. Taste to see if you need more salt. When you see the broth thickening add both chicken and beef cube. Do not let it get too thick. Put the squash in 2 parts: the first part is for it to be very soft and stringy; the second part is to be served in pieces. If you like a spicy taste you can add a few drops of Tabasco sauce. Add sour orange juice and vinegar so the Sancocho will not get dark. Yield: 18 servings.

♥ Nutritional information for this recipe is not available.

Ana Gregoria Vila, Dominican Republic

Stuffed Flounder

½ cup butter cracker crumbs
2 tablespoons melted butter
6 ounces crab meat
Salt to taste
½ teaspoon pepper
4   4-ounce flounder filets
1 cup thick white sauce

Mix cracker crumbs and butter in bowl. Add crab meat, salt and pepper; mix well. Spoon onto fish filets. Roll filets to enclose filling; arrange in 9x13-inch baking dish. Top with white sauce. Bake, covered, at 350 degrees for 15 to 20 minutes or until fish flakes easily. May prepare in individual ramekins if preferred. Yield: 4 servings.

♥ **Approx Per Serving:** Cal 351; Prot 34 g; Carbo 14 g; Fiber <1 g; T Fat 19 g; 47% Calories from Fat; Chol 128 mg; Sod 589 mg.

Dorothy E. Smerdon, Massachusetts

Baked Stuffed Haddock Casserole

3 tablespoons flour
3 tablespoons melted butter
1 cup milk
2 tablespoons fresh lemon juice
2 teaspoons grated lemon rind
1 teaspoon salt
⅛ teaspoon pepper
2 pounds fresh haddock filets
30 butter crackers, crushed
¼ cup melted butter

Blend flour into 3 tablespoons melted butter in saucepan. Cook over low heat for several minutes. Stir in milk gradually. Cook until thickened, stirring constantly. Add lemon juice, lemon rind, salt and pepper. Pour over fish in 1½ to 2-quart baking dish. Top with mixture of cracker crumbs and ¼ cup melted butter. Bake at 350 degrees for 30 minutes or just until fish flakes easily; do not overbake. Yield: 6 servings.

♥ **Approx Per Serving:** Cal 374; Prot 35 g; Carbo 16 g; Fiber <1 g; T Fat 21 g; 48% Calories from Fat; Chol 131 mg; Sod 741 mg.

Denise Haley Abplanalp, Massachusetts

Halibut Filets

This is an old Spanish recipe.

4 cups water
1 green bell pepper
1 medium onion
4 cloves of garlic
2 bay leaves
1/2 teaspoon fennel seed
1 envelope fish-flavored bouillon
  mix
2 large potatoes, sliced
1 pound halibut filets

Combine water, green pepper, onion, garlic, bay leaves, fennel seed and bouillon in saucepan. Cook until stock is of desired consistency. Strain stock. Combine potatoes with strained stock in saucepan. Cook over medium heat until potatoes are tender. Add halibut. Cook for 10 minutes or until fish flakes easily; discard bay leaves. Spoon fish and potatoes into bowls. Add stock as desired. Yield: 4 servings.

♥ **Approx Per Serving:** Cal 202; Prot 26 g; Carbo 19 g; Fiber 2 g;
  T Fat 3 g; 13% Calories from Fat; Chol 37 mg; Sod 356 mg.

Mr. and Mrs. A.R. de Arellano, Puerto Rico

Filets of Salmon en Papillote

2 pounds salmon filets
Salt and pepper to taste
8 large white mushrooms, finely
  chopped
1 bunch scallions, finely chopped
1 bunch fresh dill, finely chopped
6 tablespoons butter
1 cup dry white wine

Line 9x13-inch baking pan with enough foil to seal over fish. Sprinkle fish with salt and pepper; place in prepared pan. Sprinkle with mushrooms, scallions and dill; dot with butter. Pour wine into pan. Seal foil tightly. Bake at 350 degrees for 1 hour without opening foil.
Yield: 6 servings.

♥ **Approx Per Serving:** Cal 400; Prot 34 g; Carbo 3 g; Fiber 1 g;
  T Fat 25 g; 56% Calories from Fat; Chol 136 mg; Sod 181 mg.

Mrs. Robert Goldman, California

Salmon Steaks with Mustard Crust

2   8-ounce salmon steaks
Pepper to taste
2 tablespoons Provençale or
   tarragon mustard

Sprinkle salmon with pepper; coat with mustard. Cook in heated ovenproof 10-inch skillet over high heat for 2 minutes. Turn steaks and spread top with mustard. Bake at 500 degrees for 8 minutes. Yield: 2 servings.

♥ **Approx Per Serving:** Cal 402; Prot 50 g; Carbo 1 g; Fiber <1 g;
   T Fat 21 g; 47% Calories from Fat; Chol 158 mg; Sod 315 mg.

Mark L. Silverman, M.D., Massachusetts

Thai Swordfish

Thanks to Argaard Pinsuvana for sharing the art of Thai cooking with me. The secret is to use fresh spices and not to burn the garlic.

4 ounces teriyaki sauce
4   8-ounce swordfish steaks
2 onions
1 tablespoon sesame oil
1/3 cup water
3 scallions, chopped
1 tablespoon chopped garlic
1 red bell pepper, thinly sliced
1 cup trimmed snow peas
1 cup shiitake mushrooms
2 tablespoons chopped gingerroot
1 tablespoon sesame oil
2 tablespoons butter
1/2 cup fresh cilantro

Spoon a small amount of teriyaki sauce into shallow dish. Score both sides of fish 1/4 inch deep. Place in prepared dish; spoon remaining sauce over top. Marinate, covered, in refrigerator overnight. Cut onions into quarters and separate layers. Sauté in 1 tablespoon sesame oil in 14-inch skillet for 5 minutes or until tender. Add next 8 ingredients. Cook over medium heat for 5 minutes or until tender; do not overcook. Heat butter in cast-iron skillet over high heat. Add swordfish. Cook for 4 minutes on each side or until seared dark brown and cooked through. Place on serving plate; top with vegetables and cilantro. Yield: 4 servings.

♥ **Approx Per Serving:** Cal 531; Prot 52 g; Carbo 31 g; Fiber 9 g;
   T Fat 23 g; 38% Calories from Fat; Chol 106 mg; Sod 1354 mg.

Maxwell Lazinger, M.D., Massachusetts

Tasty Tuna Pasta

1 16-ounce package pasta shells
1/2 teaspoon oil
1 12-ounce and 1 6-ounce can
  white tuna in water, drained
Salad vinegar to taste
1/3 cup light mayonnaise-type salad
  dressing
1/2 small onion, chopped
1 teaspoon pepper
1 small tomato, chopped
Pepper to taste

Cook pasta using package directions; drain and rinse with cool water. Stir in oil. Combine tuna, vinegar, salad dressing, onion and 1 teaspoon pepper in bowl. Add pasta; mix gently. Top with tomato and additional pepper to taste.
Yield: 6 servings.

♥ **Approx Per Serving:** Cal 431; Prot 35 g; Carbo 60 g; Fiber 4 g;
  T Fat 4 g; 9% Calories from Fat; Chol 51 mg; Sod 372 mg.

Betsy Mazzoleni, New Hampshire

Grilled Wahoo Steaks

4 1 to 1 1/2-inch thick wahoo steaks
1 cup white wine
1 cup mayonnaise
Juice of 1 lemon
2 teaspoons Worcestershire sauce
Hot pepper sauce to taste
1/2 teaspoon paprika
Salt and pepper to taste

Marinate wahoo steaks in wine in bowl in refrigerator for 2 hours. Combine mayonnaise, lemon juice, Worcestershire sauce, pepper sauce, paprika, salt and pepper in bowl; mix well. Drain fish. Spread with some of the mayonnaise mixture. Grill over hot coals for 10 minutes on each side, basting occasionally with remaining mayonnaise mixture. Garnish with parsley and lemon wedges. Serve with baked potatoes and corn on the cob. Yield: 4 servings.

♥ **Approx Per Serving:** Cal 676; Prot 22 g; Carbo 3 g; Fiber <1 g;
  T Fat 60 g; 84% Calories from Fat; Chol 101 mg; Sod 415 mg.
  Nutritional information includes entire amount of wine marinade.

Mr. and Mrs. William Frith, Bermuda

Superbly Simple Island-Style Fish Filets

1/4 cup flour
1 teaspoon paprika
1/2 teaspoon salt
1/4 teaspoon freshly ground pepper
1 1/2 pounds firm grouper filets
1/2 cup butter
1 cup dry white wine
1/4 cup lemon juice
1/4 cup packed dark brown sugar
1 teaspoon ginger
1/2 cup sliced or slivered almonds
2 bananas, cut into halves
    lengthwise and crosswise

Mix flour, paprika, salt and pepper in plastic bag. Add filets 1 at a time, shaking to coat well. Shake off excess and place on platter. Chill for 1 to 8 hours. Sauté fish in butter in large skillet over medium-high heat for 3 minutes on each side. Remove to ovenproof platter; keep warm in 200-degree oven. Add wine, lemon juice, brown sugar, ginger and almonds to drippings in skillet. Bring to a boil over medium heat. Add bananas. Cook for 2 minutes, turning to coat well. Spoon bananas and sauce over fish. Serve with rice. May substitute sole or flounder for grouper.
Yield: 4 servings.

♥ **Approx Per Serving:** Cal 651; Prot 41 g; Carbo 40 g; Fiber 3 g; T Fat 34 g; 48% Calories from Fat; Chol 118 mg; Sod 567 mg.

Barbara Elkind, Florida

Italian Clam Sauce

1 cup clams, minced
1 clove of garlic, chopped
2 tablespoons oil
1 16-ounce can Italian plum
    tomatoes, drained
1/2 small hot cherry pepper,
    chopped
Salt and pepper to taste

Drain clams, reserving liquid. Sauté garlic in oil in saucepan. Add tomatoes, hot pepper, reserved clam liquid, salt and pepper. Simmer for 30 minutes. Add clams. Simmer just until cooked through; do not overcook. Serve over spaghetti.
Yield: 4 servings.

♥ **Approx Per Serving:** Cal 115; Prot 7 g; Carbo 6 g; Fiber 1 g; T Fat 8 g; 57% Calories from Fat; Chol 14 mg; Sod 208 mg.
Nutritional information does not include spaghetti.

Roberta M. Robinson, Massachusetts

Linguine with Clam Sauce

2 7-ounce cans minced clams
1 medium onion, chopped
2 cloves of garlic, chopped
2 tablespoons chopped red bell
  pepper
1 tablespoon olive oil
2 tablespoons finely chopped
  parsley
Juice of 1 lemon
1/4 teaspoon pepper
1 16-ounce package linguine
2 tablespoons grated Parmesan
  cheese

Drain clams, reserving liquid. Sauté onion, garlic and bell pepper in olive oil in medium skillet for 2 to 3 minutes. Add reserved clam liquid. Cook for 10 minutes or until liquid is reduced by 1/2. Add clams, parsley, lemon juice and pepper; mix well. Simmer for 5 minutes. Cook linguine using package directions; drain. Combine with clam mixture in bowl; toss to mix well. Sprinkle with cheese. May substitute oysters for clams and 1/4 cup white wine or vinegar for clam liquid.
Yield: 4 servings.

♥ **Approx Per Serving:** Cal 531; Prot 24 g; Carbo 93 g; Fiber 6 g; T Fat 13 g; 20% Calories from Fat; Chol 65 mg; Sod 93 mg.

Susana R. Alvarez, M.D., Massachusetts

Broiled Crawfish

6 large crawfish, boiled
2 large onions, chopped
1 green bell pepper, chopped
4 cloves of garlic, chopped
1 cup olive oil
1 cup chopped fresh or canned
  tomatoes
1/2 cup bread crumbs
1/2 cup grated Parmesan cheese
2 tablespoons butter

Split crawfish shells from head to tail. Remove and chop meat, reserving shells. Sauté onions, green pepper and garlic in olive oil in skillet until light brown. Add tomatoes. Simmer for 30 minutes. Stir in bread crumbs and crawfish meat. Spoon into shells. Place on rack in broiler pan. Sprinkle with cheese; dot with butter. Broil until brown.
Yield: 6 servings.

♥ **Approx Per Serving:** Cal 495; Prot 16 g; Carbo 13 g; Fiber 2 g; T Fat 43 g; 77% Calories from Fat; Chol 93 mg; Sod 253 mg.

Richard Murray, New York

Lobster Spaghetti Sauce

3   1½-pound live lobsters
2   cups water
2   29-ounce cans tomato purée
¼   teaspoon minced garlic
¼   cup olive oil
2   teaspoons sugar
2   teaspoons salt
3   16-ounce packages spaghetti,
    cooked, drained

Break lobsters into claws, tails and bodies; rinse with cold water. Combine with next 6 ingredients in saucepan. Simmer, covered, for 2 to 2½ hours. Simmer, uncovered, for 30 minutes or until thickened. Remove lobsters from sauce and remove meat. Serve sauce over pasta; serve lobster separately. Yield: 12 servings.

♥ **Approx Per Serving:** Cal 584; Prot 30 g; Carbo 101 g; Fiber 8 g;
  T Fat 6 g; 10% Calories from Fat; Chol 49 mg; Sod 643 mg.

Donald Cappadona, M.D., Massachusetts

White Wine-Scallop Lasagna

1 cup chopped green onions
1 clove of garlic, minced
½ teaspoon chopped fresh thyme
  or ¾ teaspoon dried thyme
1 tablespoon butter
2 pounds scallops, cut into ½-inch
  pieces
⅓ cup flour
7 tablespoons melted butter
1 cup chicken broth
1 cup whipping cream
½ cup white wine or dry vermouth
1   16-ounce package lasagna
    noodles, cooked, drained
2 cups shredded Swiss cheese

Sauté first 3 ingredients in 1 table-spoon butter in skillet over medium-high heat for 1 minute. Add scallops. Stir-fry until opaque in center. Strain over bowl for 20 minutes. Reduce scallop liquid in saucepan to 2 tablespoons. Cook flour with 7 tablespoons melted butter in skillet until light brown, stirring constantly; remove from heat. Stir in broth, cream and wine. Cook over high heat until thickened, stirring constantly. Stir in reduced liquid. Layer noodles, sauce, scallops and cheese ⅓ at a time in large baking dish. Chill, covered, for 24 hours. Bake, covered, at 350 degrees for 20 minutes. Bake, uncovered, for 20 minutes. Let stand for 15 minutes before serving. Yield: 6 servings.

♥ **Approx Per Serving:** Cal 896; Prot 52 g; Carbo 70 g; Fiber 1 g;
  T Fat 44 g; 45% Calories from Fat; Chol 184 mg; Sod 618 mg.

Sheila Veidenheimer, Massachusetts

Char Koay Teow

This is a spicy version of fast food from the Malay Island of Penang. It is cooked and served from hawkers' pushcarts on the streets. Koay Teow are flat Chinese rice noodles. You may vary the amount of chili powder to suit your tastes.

10 ounces koay teow or rice noodles
2 cloves of garlic, finely chopped
2 tablespoons lard
5 ounces peeled small or medium
  shrimp
5 ounces bean sprouts
2 tablespoons chili powder
2 tablespoons soy sauce
4 eggs, beaten
5 chive stems, cut into 1-inch pieces

Soak rice noodles in warm water in bowl until soft but not soggy; drain. Sauté garlic in lard in wok. Drain, reserving drippings; discard garlic. Heat reserved garlic-oil in wok. Add shrimp, bean sprouts, rice noodles, chili powder and soy sauce. Stir-fry until shrimp are cooked through. Add eggs. Stir-fry until cooked through. Add chives. Stir-fry until heated through. Yield: 4 servings.

♥ **Approx Per Serving:** Cal 460; Prot 19 g; Carbo 64 g; Fiber 4 g;
  T Fat 14 g; 28% Calories from Fat; Chol 274 mg; Sod 694 mg.

Winnie Ooi, M.D., Massachusetts

Shrimp Creole

2 medium onions, thinly sliced
1 medium green bell pepper, cut
  into thin strips
4 ounces fresh mushrooms, sliced
1/4 cup oil
1/4 cup flour
1 teaspoon oregano
1 teaspoon salt
1/4 teaspoon pepper
2 1/2 cups stewed tomatoes
1/2 cup tomato juice
1 to 1 1/2 pounds cooked shrimp

Sauté onions, green pepper and mushrooms in oil in saucepan until vegetables are tender. Stir in flour, oregano, salt and pepper. Add tomatoes. Cook until thickened, stirring constantly. Simmer, covered, for 10 minutes. Stir in tomato juice and shrimp. Simmer for 5 minutes. Serve over cooked rice with a crisp green salad. Yield: 4 servings.

♥ **Approx Per Serving:** Cal 405; Prot 40 g; Carbo 27 g; Fiber 3 g;
  T Fat 16 g; 35% Calories from Fat; Chol 332 mg; Sod 1478 mg.

Ann C. Heffernon, Massachusetts

Linguine with Shrimp and Bread Crumbs

4¹/₂ ounces uncooked linguine
2 tablespoons grated Parmesan
  cheese
2 teaspoons olive oil
¹/₂ ounce anchovy filets
2 teaspoons olive oil
2 ounces day-old Italian bread,
  coarsely crumbled
2 cloves of garlic, minced
¹/₄ teaspoon dried red pepper flakes
24 medium shrimp, peeled,
  deveined
2 tablespoons chopped fresh
  parsley

Cook linguine in boiling water in large saucepan for 8 minutes or just until tender; drain. Combine with cheese and 2 teaspoons olive oil in serving bowl; keep warm. Sauté anchovies in 2 teaspoons oil in nonstick skillet for 2 to 3 minutes. Add bread crumbs, garlic and pepper flakes. Cook for 4 minutes or until bread crumbs are brown, stirring constantly. Add to linguine. Add shrimp to skillet. Sauté for 4 minutes or until shrimp turn pink. Add to linguine; toss gently. Sprinkle with parsley. Yield: 4 servings.

● **Approx Per Serving:** Cal 249; Prot 14 g; Carbo 33 g; Fiber 2 g;
  T Fat 6 g; 24% Calories from Fat; Chol 61 mg; Sod 330 mg.

Marie C. Ludwick, Florida

Shrimp Casserole

2 cups cooked shrimp
2 cups cream of mushroom soup
1 cup sour cream
1 cup sliced mushrooms, cooked
1/2 tablespoon dry mustard
1/2 cup grated Parmesan cheese
1 pound spinach, cooked

Combine shrimp, soup, sour cream, mushrooms, dry mustard and cheese in bowl; mix well. Alternate layers of shrimp mixture and spinach in baking dish until all ingredients are used. Bake at 350 degrees for 30 minutes. Yield: 4 servings.

💜 **Approx Per Serving:** Cal 407; Prot 29 g; Carbo 17 g; Fiber 4 g; T Fat 26 g; 56% Calories from Fat; Chol 193 mg; Sod 1507 mg.

Gretchen Stone Cook, Massachusetts

Shrimp Scampi

1 pound shrimp, cleaned
1/4 cup butter, melted
1/2 cup oil
3 cloves of garlic
1 teaspoon chopped fresh parsley
1/4 cup white wine
1/4 cup grated Parmesan cheese

Arrange shrimp in single layer in mixture of butter and oil in baking dish. Add mixture of garlic, parsley and white wine. Sprinkle with cheese. Bake at 400 degrees for 15 minutes. Discard garlic. Serve over linguine. Yield: 4 servings.

💜 **Approx Per Serving:** Cal 459; Prot 19 g; Carbo 1 g; Fiber <1 g; T Fat 41 g; 82% Calories from Fat; Chol 193 mg; Sod 374 mg.

Patricia Toye, Massachusetts

Tasty Grilled Shrimp

1 pound fresh large shrimp in
   shells, rinsed, drained
1/2 cup oil
1/2 cup fresh lemon juice
1/4 cup reduced-sodium soy sauce
Pepper to taste
1/4 cup thinly sliced green onions

Marinate shrimp in mixture of next 4 ingredients in bowl for 30 minutes. Remove shrimp; reserve marinade. Grill over medium coals for 10 minutes, turning and brushing with marinade. Serve with mixture of marinade and onions. Yield: 2 servings.

💜 **Approx Per Serving:** Cal 672; Prot 34 g; Carbo 9 g; Fiber 1 g; T Fat 56 g; 75% Calories from Fat; Chol 316 mg; Sod 1146 mg.

Brenda Nieh, Massachusetts

Seafood Casserole

1 cup chopped onion
3 cups chopped celery
3 tablespoons butter
1 teaspoon salt
1/4 teaspoon pepper
5 cups milk
3/4 cup flour
1/2 cup melted butter
1 pound Velveeta cheese, chopped
1   10-ounce can lobster meat, drained
1   7-ounce can crab meat, drained
1 pound cooked shrimp
1 pound scallops, cut into quarters, cooked

Sauté onion and celery in 3 tablespoons butter in skillet. Add salt and pepper. Bring milk to a boil in small saucepan. Blend flour into 1/2 cup melted butter in large saucepan. Stir in hot milk. Cook until thickened, stirring constantly. Stir in cheese until melted. Add sautéed vegetables, lobster, crab meat, shrimp and scallops; mix gently. Spoon into baking dish. Bake at 350 degrees for 30 minutes. Serve with baked potatoes or rice and lettuce and tomato salad. Yield: 8 servings.

♥ **Approx Per Serving:** Cal 667; Prot 53 g; Carbo 22 g; Fiber 1 g; T Fat 40 g; 55% Calories from Fat; Chol 295 mg; Sod 1748 mg.

Mariette Theriault, Canada

Scallops Chappaquiddick

3 slices bread
2 cloves of garlic, minced
Chopped parsley to taste
1/2 cup butter
1 cup crushed butter crackers
1 pound scallops
1/2 to 1 cup light cream
Salt and pepper to taste

Process bread in blender container until crumbs. Sauté garlic and parsley in butter in skillet. Stir in bread crumbs and cracker crumbs. Alternate layers of crumb mixture and scallops in baking dish until all ingredients are used. Add cream, salt and pepper. Bake at 350 degrees for 25 minutes or until scallops are cooked through. Serve immediately. Yield: 4 servings.

♥ **Approx Per Serving:** Cal 644; Prot 26 g; Carbo 30 g; Fiber 1 g; T Fat 50 g; 67% Calories from Fat; Chol 168 mg; Sod 711 mg.

Rosita Japlit, Massachusetts

Side Dishes
&
Breads

Baked Beans

2   16-ounce cans pork and beans,
        drained, rinsed
3/4 cup packed light brown sugar
1/2 cup catsup
1 small onion, minced
3 slices bacon, cut into halves
1/2 cup dark molasses
1 teaspoon dry mustard

Drain and rinse beans. Combine with brown sugar, catsup, onion, bacon, molasses and dry mustard in bowl; mix well. Spoon into bean pot. Bake, covered, at 350 degrees for 45 minutes. Yield: 6 servings.

♥ **Approx Per Serving:** Cal 402; Prot 10 g; Carbo 87 g; Fiber 9 g;
    T Fat 4 g; 8% Calories from Fat; Chol 13 mg; Sod 836 mg.

Beverly Woodford, Massachusetts

Bean Medley

1 large onion, chopped
2 stalks celery, chopped
1 medium green bell pepper,
        chopped
3 tablespoons oil
1   28-ounce can red kidney beans,
        drained
1   10-ounce package frozen lima
        beans, thawed
2   10-ounce cans no-salt-added
        tomatoes
1 1/2 cups quick-cooking barley
2/3 cup chopped parsley
2 cloves of garlic, minced
Oregano to taste
1 teaspoon basil
Salt to taste
1/2 teaspoon pepper
2 cups boiling water

Sauté onion, celery and green pepper in oil in skillet over high heat for 10 minutes. Stir in kidney beans, lima beans, tomatoes, barley, parsley, garlic, oregano, basil, salt and pepper. Spoon into 9x13-inch baking dish. Stir in boiling water. Bake, covered, at 350 degrees for 1 to 1 1/2 hours or until barley is tender, stirring frequently. Yield: 6 servings.

♥ **Approx Per Serving:** Cal 433; Prot 16 g; Carbo 78 g; Fiber 23 g;
    T Fat 8 g; 16% Calories from Fat; Chol 0 mg; Sod 508 mg.

Carol Von Ette, New Hampshire

Green Beans Wrapped in Bacon

1 pound green beans
6 slices bacon

Cook beans in water in saucepan until tender-crisp; drain and cool. Cut bacon into halves. Fry in skillet until limp; drain. Arrange beans in bunches of 10 or 12. Wrap each bunch in bacon; secure with wooden picks. Arrange in 8x10-inch baking pan. Bake at 350 degrees for 20 to 30 minutes or until beans are heated through and bacon is crisp.
Yield: 6 servings.

♥ **Approx Per Serving:** Cal 60; Prot 3 g; Carbo 5 g; Fiber 2 g; T Fat 3 g; 45% Calories from Fat; Chol 5 mg; Sod 105 mg.

Bill MacKay, New Hampshire

Grandma's Hungarian Cabbage and Noodle Delight

1 onion
1 head cabbage
2 tablespoons (or more) oil
1   16-ounce package wide noodles, cooked
Salt to taste

Grate the onion and cabbage by hand or in food processor. Pat with paper towels to dry. Sauté in several small batches in oil in skillet until brown, adding additional oil as necessary. Combine with noodles and salt in bowl; mix well.
Yield: 8 servings.

♥ **Approx Per Serving:** Cal 264; Prot 9 g; Carbo 43 g; Fiber 1 g; T Fat 6 g; 22% Calories from Fat; Chol 100 mg; Sod 15 mg.

Phyllis Steinberg, Massachusetts

Carrots Piedmontese

1 pound carrots, peeled, thinly
　　sliced
Salt to taste
3 tablespoons margarine
1 small onion, very thinly sliced
1 small clove of garlic
1/2 teaspoon salt
1 tablespoon light vinegar
1 tablespoon chopped chives

Cook carrots, covered, in boiling salted water in saucepan for 3 minutes; drain. Combine carrots with margarine, onion, garlic and 1/2 teaspoon salt in saucepan; mix well. Cook, covered, over low heat for 10 minutes. Discard garlic. Stir in vinegar. Spoon into serving dish; sprinkle with chives.
Yield: 8 servings.

♥ **Approx Per Serving:** Cal 68; Prot 1 g; Carbo 7 g; Fiber 2 g;
　　T Fat 4 g; 56% Calories from Fat; Chol 0 mg; Sod 203 mg.

Carol Baffi Dugan, Massachusetts

Zesty Carrots

6 large carrots, sliced or julienned
2 tablespoons horseradish
2 tablespoons grated onion
1/2 cup mayonnaise
Salt and pepper to taste

Cook carrots in a small amount of water in saucepan until tender-crisp; drain, reserving 1/4 cup cooking liquid. Combine reserved liquid with horseradish, onion, mayonnaise, salt and pepper in bowl. Stir in carrots. Spoon into baking dish. Bake at 350 degrees just until heated through. May top with mixture of bread crumbs and 2 tablespoons melted butter if desired. May adjust the amount of onion and horseradish to suit individual tastes.
Yield: 8 servings.

♥ **Approx Per Serving:** Cal 124; Prot 1 g; Carbo 6 g; Fiber 2 g;
　　T Fat 11 g; 78% Calories from Fat; Chol 8 mg; Sod 100 mg.

James P. Burke, M.D., Massachusetts

Cheesy Eggplant Casserole

1 eggplant
1 onion, chopped
1 green bell pepper, chopped
2 tablespoons butter
1 tablespoon flour
1 teaspoon oregano
Salt and pepper to taste
1   10-ounce can cream of
    mushroom soup
3 eggs, beaten
1 cup shredded cheese
1 cup bread crumbs
2 tablespoons melted butter

Peel eggplant and cut into cubes. Cook in boiling water in saucepan for 15 minutes; drain. Sauté onion and green pepper in 2 tablespoons butter in saucepan until tender. Stir in flour, oregano, salt and pepper. Add soup. Cook until bubbly; remove from heat. Stir in eggs, cheese and eggplant. Spoon into 10x10-inch baking dish. Top with mixture of bread crumbs and 2 tablespoons melted butter. Bake at 350 degrees for 35 minutes. Yield: 8 servings.

♥ **Approx Per Serving:** Cal 244; Prot 8 g; Carbo 17 g; Fiber 2 g;
  T Fat 16 g; 59% Calories from Fat; Chol 135 mg; Sod 541 mg.

Anne Abbruzzese, Massachusetts

Eggplant Balls

1 medium eggplant
3/4 cup shredded sharp Cheddar
    cheese
1 egg, beaten
1/2 cup finely chopped pepperoni
3/4 cup Italian bread crumbs
Salt and pepper to taste
1/2 cup flour
2 tablespoons (about) oil

Peel eggplant and cut into cubes. Cook in water to cover in saucepan for 10 to 15 minutes or until tender; drain. Mash eggplant in large bowl. Add cheese, egg, pepperoni, bread crumbs, salt and pepper; mix well. Shape into small balls. Coat with flour. Brown a few at a time in oil in skillet; drain on paper towels. May chill mixture before forming balls for easier handling. Yield: 8 servings.

♥ **Approx Per Serving:** Cal 229; Prot 9 g; Carbo 16 g; Fiber 2 g;
  T Fat 14 g; 57% Calories from Fat; Chol 43 mg; Sod 434 mg.

Ann DeVito, Massachusetts

Breakfast Potatoes

2 cups chopped potatoes
4 slices bacon, crisp-fried
2 eggs, beaten
Salt and pepper to taste

Cook potatoes in nonstick skillet sprayed with nonstick cooking spray until golden brown. Top with bacon. Pour eggs over top; sprinkle with salt and pepper. Cook until eggs are set. Yield: 4 servings.

♥ **Approx Per Serving:** Cal 134; Prot 6 g; Carbo 14 g; Fiber 1 g; T Fat 6 g; 40% Calories from Fat; Chol 112 mg; Sod 139 mg.

Kay Klimarchuk, Massachusetts

Mrs. Quigley's Potato Casserole

1   32-ounce package frozen hashed brown potatoes, thawed
1   10-ounce can cream of chicken soup
2 cups sour cream
8 ounces Cheddar cheese, shredded
1 cup crushed butter crackers
1/4 cup melted butter

Combine potatoes, soup, sour cream and cheese in bowl; mix well. Spoon into large baking dish. Top with cracker crumbs; drizzle with butter. Bake at 350 degrees for 1 1/4 hours. Yield: 8 servings.

♥ **Approx Per Serving:** Cal 621; Prot 14 g; Carbo 45 g; Fiber 2 g; T Fat 46 g; 64% Calories from Fat; Chol 74 mg; Sod 677 mg.

Deborah Quigley, Massachusetts

My trip to Romania has had an immense impact on my life. The blessings and love the children gave back to us will never be forgotten.

—Anne Reilly, C.P.N.P.
Lahey Holliston Pediatrics

Party Mashed Potatoes

10 medium potatoes
2 tablespoons butter
6 ounces cream cheese, softened
1 cup sour cream
1 teaspoon onion salt
1 teaspoon garlic salt
1/4 teaspoon freshly ground pepper

Peel potatoes and cut into quarters. Cook in water to cover in large saucepan for 20 to 25 minutes or until tender; drain. Mash with butter in bowl until smooth. Combine cream cheese, sour cream, onion salt, garlic salt and pepper in small bowl; mix well. Add to potatoes; whisk until smooth and fluffy. Spoon into 2-quart baking dish. Bake at 350 degrees for 30 to 45 minutes or until heated through. May top with shredded cheese or paprika if desired. May substitute plain yogurt for sour cream. Yield: 10 servings.

♥ **Approx Per Serving:** Cal 246; Prot 4 g; Carbo 29 g; Fiber 2 g; T Fat 13 g; 47% Calories from Fat; Chol 35 mg; Sod 453 mg.

Ruth Joslyn, Massachusetts

Potato Casserole

6 medium potatoes
1   10-ounce can cream of chicken soup
1/4 to 1/2 cup butter
2 cups sour cream
1/2 cup chopped green onions
11/2 cups shredded Cheddar cheese
1 cup crushed cornflakes
1 tablespoon melted butter

Cook potatoes in water in saucepan until tender; drain and cool. Peel and grate potatoes. Heat soup with 1/4 cup butter in saucepan, stirring until smooth. Stir in sour cream, green onions and cheese. Add potatoes; mix well. Spoon into buttered 4-quart baking dish. Top with mixture of cornflakes and 1 tablespoon melted butter. Bake at 350 degrees for 45 minutes. Serve with chicken and French bread. Yield: 6 servings.

♥ **Approx Per Serving:** Cal 637; Prot 14 g; Carbo 44 g; Fiber 3 g; T Fat 46 g; 64% Calories from Fat; Chol 114 mg; Sod 881 mg.

Kelly Maloney, Massachusetts

Potatoes Dianna

6 large potatoes, peeled, shredded
1¹/₂ cups shredded Cheddar cheese
¹/₂ cup sour cream
1 large onion, chopped
¹/₂ cup butter
Garlic powder, salt and pepper to
    taste
¹/₂ cup shredded Cheddar cheese
¹/₂ cup grated Parmesan cheese

Combine potatoes with 1¹/₂ cups Cheddar cheese and sour cream in bowl; mix well. Sauté onion in butter in skillet until tender. Add to potatoes; mix gently. Season with garlic powder, salt and pepper. Spoon into large baking pan. Top with remaining ¹/₂ cup Cheddar cheese and Parmesan cheese. Bake at 375 degrees for 30 minutes.
Yield: 8 servings.

♥ **Approx Per Serving:** Cal 363; Prot 12 g; Carbo 23 g; Fiber 2 g;
    T Fat 26 g; 62% Calories from Fat; Chol 71 mg; Sod 380 mg.

Midge Giodano, Massachusetts

Three-Cheese and Spinach Pie

1   10-ounce package frozen
    chopped spinach
6 eggs
3 ounces cream cheese, softened
¹/₄ cup shredded Cheddar cheese
2 tablespoons sliced green onions
1 tablespoon chopped parsley
¹/₂ teaspoon salt
Pepper to taste
1 unbaked 10-inch pie shell
2 tablespoons grated Parmesan
    cheese

Cook spinach using package directions; drain well. Combine eggs, cream cheese and Cheddar cheese in bowl; mix well. Add spinach, green onions, parsley, salt and pepper; mix well. Spoon into pie shell; top with Parmesan cheese. Bake at 425 degrees for 20 to 25 minutes or until edge is set. Let stand for 10 minutes before serving. Yield: 6 servings.

♥ **Approx Per Serving:** Cal 336; Prot 13 g; Carbo 18 g; Fiber 2 g;
    T Fat 24 g; 63% Calories from Fat; Chol 235 mg; Sod 594 mg.

Valerie Heemstra, Massachusetts

Sweet Potato and Pineapple Soufflé

3 cups mashed cooked sweet
  potatoes
3 tablespoons butter
1/2 teaspoon grated lemon rind
2 egg yolks, beaten
1/2 teaspoon salt
1/2 to 3/4 cup drained crushed
  pineapple
2 egg whites, stiffly beaten

Combine sweet potatoes, butter, lemon rind, egg yolks and salt in bowl; beat with fork until fluffy. Stir in pineapple. Fold in egg whites gently. Spoon into greased 7-inch baking dish. Bake at 350 degrees for 40 minutes. Serve with ham. May substitute tart applesauce for pineapple. Yield: 6 servings.

♥ **Approx Per Serving:** Cal 266; Prot 5 g; Carbo 44 g; Fiber 2 g;
   T Fat 8 g; 27% Calories from Fat; Chol 87 mg; Sod 267 mg.

Marian Adderley, Bermuda

Macomber Turnip Purée

The Macomber turnip is a sweet, crisp and mild-flavored cross between a rutabaga and a radish developed by the Macomber brothers in 1876. True Macomber turnips are grown only in Westport, Massachusetts, and in the area where the sandy soils and temperate coastal New England climate are favorable for the vegetable.

3 12-ounce packages Macomber
  turnips, peeled, chopped
2 tablespoons unsalted butter,
  chopped
1 poached fresh pear or 1 canned
  pear, chopped
Salt and freshly ground pepper to
  taste
8 miniature edible pumpkins,
  seeded

Bring turnips to a boil in water to cover in saucepan; reduce heat. Simmer for 20 minutes or until very tender; drain. Combine with butter, pear, salt and pepper in blender or food processor container. Pulse until puréed. Reheat in saucepan. Spoon into pumpkins to serve. May also serve in 1 small pumpkin or use as garnish for turkey. May substitute 3 medium turnips for Macomber turnips. Yield: 8 servings.

♥ **Approx Per Serving:** Cal 97; Prot 2 g; Carbo 17 g; Fiber 5 g;
   T Fat 3 g; 27% Calories from Fat; Chol 8 mg; Sod 88 mg.

Carol Russell, Massachusetts

Italian Zucchini Crescent Pie

4 cups sliced unpeeled zucchini
1 cup chopped onion
1/4 cup margarine
2 tablespoons parsley flakes
1/4 teaspoon each garlic powder,
    basil leaves and oregano
1/2 teaspoon each salt and pepper
2 eggs
2 cups shredded mozzarella cheese
1 8-count can crescent rolls
2 teaspoons mustard

Sauté zucchini and onion in margarine in skillet for 10 minutes or just until tender. Stir in parsley flakes, garlic powder, basil, oregano, salt and pepper. Combine eggs and cheese in bowl; mix well. Stir in sautéed vegetables. Separate roll dough into 8 triangles. Arrange in ungreased 9 to 10-inch pie plate, pressing edges to seal. Spread with mustard. Spoon zucchini mixture into prepared pie plate. Bake at 375 degrees for 20 minutes or until knife inserted in center comes out clean. Let stand for 10 minutes before serving. Yield: 6 servings.

♥ **Approx Per Serving:** Cal 334; Prot 13 g; Carbo 18 g; Fiber 1 g;
    T Fat 23 g; 63% Calories from Fat; Chol 100 mg; Sod 708 mg.

Barbara Davison, Massachusetts

Zucchini Casserole

3 large zucchini, sliced
1/4 cup chopped onion
Salt to taste
1 cup sour cream
1 10-ounce can cream of chicken
    soup
1 8-ounce package stuffing mix
1/2 cup melted margarine

Cook zucchini and onion in salted water to cover in saucepan for 5 to 10 minutes or until tender; drain. Combine sour cream and soup in bowl; mix well. Add zucchini mixture; mix well. Combine stuffing mix with margarine in bowl. Spread half the stuffing mixture in 9x13-inch baking dish. Layer zucchini mixture and remaining stuffing mixture in prepared dish. Bake at 350 degrees for 30 minutes. Yield: 10 servings.

♥ **Approx Per Serving:** Cal 254; Prot 5 g; Carbo 22 g; Fiber 1 g;
    T Fat 17 g; 58% Calories from Fat; Chol 11 mg; Sod 616 mg.

Mary C. DeChiara, Massachusetts

Chinese Fettucini

¹/₂ cup sliced carrot
¹/₂ cup chopped zucchini
¹/₂ cup broccoli flowerets
¹/₂ cup snow peas
¹/₄ cup water chestnuts
2 tablespoons oil
16 ounces uncooked fresh fettucini
²/₃ 7-ounce bottle of oyster sauce

Stir-fry carrot, zucchini, broccoli, snow peas and water chestnuts in oil in wok or large skillet until tender-crisp; keep warm. Cook fettucini using package directions; drain and keep warm. Add half the oyster sauce to fettucini in large serving platter; mix well. Add stir-fried vegetables and remaining oyster sauce; mix well. May add chicken breast filet, shrimp or scallops or vary vegetables to suit individual tastes. May substitute frozen mixed Japanese vegetables for fresh vegetables. Yield: 4 servings.

♥ **Approx Per Serving:** Cal 432; Prot 17 g; Carbo 65 g; Fiber 2 g; T Fat 11 g; 23% Calories from Fat; Chol 101 mg; Sod 49 mg. Nutritional information does not include oyster sauce.

Jo Fernandez, Massachusetts

Fettucini Verde

6 tablespoons butter, chopped
1 cup chopped green onions with tops
2 cloves of garlic, minced
4 cups cooked drained vegetable fettucini
1 cup half and half
1 cup grated Parmesan cheese
Nutmeg, salt and pepper to taste

Melt butter in wok over medium-high heat. Add green onions and garlic. Stir-fry until tender-crisp. Add pasta and half and half; mix well. Cook over high heat just until half and half comes to a boil; remove from heat. Sprinkle with cheese, nutmeg, salt and pepper; toss to mix well. Yield: 4 servings.

♥ **Approx Per Serving:** Cal 487; Prot 16 g; Carbo 37 g; Fiber 3 g; T Fat 31 g; 57% Calories from Fat; Chol 85 mg; Sod 549 mg.

Lynn Connors, Massachusetts

Aglio e Olio

5 or 6 large cloves of garlic
1   3-ounce can anchovies, drained
1 cup olive oil
1/2 cup fresh parsley
1/2 cup fresh basil
1/2 teaspoon red pepper
1 teaspoon black pepper
1   16-ounce package linguine,
     cooked
1/2 cup grated Romano cheese

*P*rocess garlic and anchovies in food processor until smooth. Sauté in olive oil in skillet for 5 to 7 minutes or until bubbly. Process parsley and basil in food processor until smooth. Add to skillet with red pepper and black pepper. Simmer for 5 minutes longer. Add to linguine; toss to mix well. Sprinkle with cheese. Yield: 8 servings.

♥ **Approx Per Serving:** Cal 502; Prot 13 g; Carbo 45 g; Fiber 3 g;
   T Fat 31 g; 56% Calories from Fat; Chol 6 mg; Sod 465 mg.

Lisa G. Polacke, New Hampshire

Apricot Kugel

1   16-ounce package medium egg
     noodles
5 eggs
1 cup melted margarine
1 cup orange juice
1   12-ounce jar apricot preserves
1/4 cup graham cracker crumbs
1   16-ounce can apricot halves

*C*ook noodles using package directions; drain. Combine eggs, margarine, orange juice and apricot preserves in bowl; mix well. Add noodles; mix well. Spoon into greased 9x13-inch baking pan. Top with cracker crumbs and apricot halves. Bake at 350 degrees for 1 hour. May also serve as dessert. Yield: 12 servings.

♥ **Approx Per Serving:** Cal 442; Prot 9 g; Carbo 59 g; Fiber 1 g;
   T Fat 20 g; 40% Calories from Fat; Chol 155 mg; Sod 233 mg.

Barbara Kess, Massachusetts

Noodle Kugel

1 16-ounce package wide noodles
1 pound creamed cottage cheese
4 ounces Velveeta cheese, chopped
1 cup sour cream
1/2 cup melted butter
1 tablespoon (about) sugar
4 eggs
2 cups milk
1/2 cup sugar
1 teaspoon vanilla extract
Cinnamon to taste
1/4 cup sugar

Cook noodles using package directions; drain. Combine cottage cheese, Velveeta cheese, sour cream, butter and 1 tablespoon sugar in bowl; mix well. Add noodles; mix well. Spoon into 9x13-inch baking dish. Combine eggs, milk, 1/2 cup sugar and vanilla in saucepan. Cook over very low heat until sugar dissolves, stirring constantly. Pour over noodle mixture. Sprinkle with cinnamon and 1/4 cup sugar. Bake at 350 degrees for 1 to 1 1/4 hours. Yield: 10 servings.

♥ **Approx Per Serving:** Cal 519; Prot 19 g; Carbo 53 g; Fiber 0 g; T Fat 26 g; 44% Calories from Fat; Chol 224 mg; Sod 491 mg.

Sharon Steinberg, Massachusetts

Pesto Genovese for Spaghetti

1 cup loosely packed basil leaves
1/2 cup walnuts
2 cloves of garlic
3/4 cup freshly grated Parmesan
   cheese
1/2 cup olive oil

Combine basil, walnuts and garlic in blender container; process until smooth. Add cheese; process until well mixed. Add oil gradually, processing constantly at low speed. Serve or toss with pasta to serve. May substitute pine nuts for walnuts. Yield: 4 servings.

♥ **Approx Per Serving:** Cal 421; Prot 9 g; Carbo 7 g; Fiber 2 g; T Fat 41 g; 85% Calories from Fat; Chol 12 mg; Sod 287 mg.

Vinnie Zinna, Massachusetts

Baked Rice

1¼ cups uncooked rice
1 10-ounce can onion soup
1 10-ounce can consommé
½ cup margarine, softened
1 8-ounce can mushrooms

Combine rice, soup, consommé, margarine and mushrooms in bowl; mix well. Spoon into baking dish. Bake at 350 degrees for 1 to 1¼ hours or until rice is tender, stirring after 30 minutes. Yield: 8 servings.

♥ **Approx Per Serving:** Cal 238; Prot 5 g; Carbo 28 g; Fiber 1 g; T Fat 12 g; 45% Calories from Fat; Chol 0 mg; Sod 745 mg.

Jacqueline Hetnik, Massachusetts

Multi-Purpose Tomato Sauce

1 onion, sliced or chopped
3 tablespoons canola oil
2 carrots, sliced
1 bell pepper of any color, chopped
1 6-ounce jar marinated artichoke hearts, drained, chopped
4 fresh tomatoes, chopped
1 tablespoon oregano
1 tablespoon basil
2 bay leaves
2 28-ounce cans tomatoes, crushed
Salt and pepper to taste

Sauté onion in oil in large saucepan over medium heat. Add carrots. Sauté for 3 minutes. Add bell pepper and artichoke hearts. Cook for 2 minutes. Add fresh tomatoes, oregano, basil and bay leaves; mix well. Cook for 5 minutes. Stir in canned tomatoes, salt and pepper. Simmer for 30 minutes, stirring occasionally. Discard bay leaves. Use in lasagna or other recipes calling for tomato sauce. May cook longer or add tomato paste for a thicker sauce. May substitute tomato purée, plum tomatoes or tomato sauce for crushed tomatoes. May add cooked vegetables such as broccoli or cauliflower or chopped olives.
Yield: 16 (½-cup) servings.

♥ **Approx Per Serving:** Cal 67; Prot 2 g; Carbo 8 g; Fiber 3 g; T Fat 4 g; 46% Calories from Fat; Chol 0 mg; Sod 223 mg.

Julie Balaban, Massachusetts

Scalloped Oyster Stuffing

1 pint oysters
2 cups crushed unsalted crackers
1/2 cup melted margarine
1/2 teaspoon salt
1/8 teaspoon pepper
1/4 teaspoon Worcestershire sauce
1 cup 1% milk

Drain oysters, reserving liquid. Combine cracker crumbs, melted margarine, salt and pepper in bowl; mix well. Sprinkle 1/3 of the crumbs in 2-quart baking dish. Layer oysters and remaining crumbs 1/2 at a time in prepared baking dish. Combine reserved oyster liquid with Worcestershire sauce and milk in bowl; mix well. Pour over layers. Bake at 350 degrees for 30 minutes or until brown. Yield: 8 servings.

💜 **Approx Per Serving:** Cal 268; Prot 10 g; Carbo 17 g; Fiber 4 g; T Fat 69 g; 86% Calories from Fat; Chol 268 mg; Sod 585 mg.

Cathy Mandel, Massachusetts

Baked Stuffed Pumpkin

1   4 to 5-pound pumpkin
2 tablespoons melted butter
2 to 3 tablespoons sugar
2 cups milk, scalded
1/3 cup sugar
1/4 cup butter
2 cups stale bread cubes
3 eggs
2/3 cup raisins
1/4 teaspoon salt
1 teaspoon cinnamon
1/2 teaspoon nutmeg

Wash pumpkin; dry. Cut off top; reserve. Remove seeds from pumpkin; discard. Place pumpkin on baking sheet. Brush inside with melted butter; sprinkle with 2 to 3 tablespoons sugar. Bake at 350 degrees for 20 minutes. Pour mixture of next 3 ingredients over bread in bowl. Let stand for 5 minutes. Beat eggs in mixer bowl. Add raisins, salt and spices. Add to bread mixture; mix well. Spoon into pumpkin. Bake for 1 1/2 to 1 3/4 hours or until custard is set. Custard will puff up and fall as it cools. Let stand for 10 minutes before serving. Add top. Yield: 8 servings.

💜 **Approx Per Serving:** Cal 275; Prot 6 g; Carbo 36 g; Fiber 3 g; T Fat 13 g; 41% Calories from Fat; Chol 111 mg; Sod 232 mg.

Bill Hamilton, New Hampshire

Blueberry and Sausage Breakfast Cake

1 pound bulk sausage
2 cups flour
1 teaspoon baking powder
1/2 teaspoon baking soda
1/2 cup margarine, softened
3/4 cup sugar
1/4 cup packed brown sugar
2 eggs
1 cup sour cream
1 cup blueberries
1/2 cup chopped pecans
1/2 cup sugar
2 tablespoons cornstarch
1/2 cup water
2 cups blueberries
1/2 teaspoon lemon juice

Brown sausage in skillet, stirring until crumbly; drain. Mix flour, baking powder and baking soda in medium bowl. Cream margarine at medium speed in mixer bowl until fluffy. Add 3/4 cup sugar and brown sugar, beating until light. Add eggs 1 at a time, beating for 1 minute after each addition. Add flour mixture alternately with sour cream, mixing just until moistened after each addition. Fold in sausage and 1 cup blueberries. Spread evenly in ungreased 9x13-inch baking pan; sprinkle with pecans. Bake at 350 degrees for 35 to 40 minutes or until wooden pick comes out clean. Mix 1/2 cup sugar and cornstarch in medium saucepan. Stir in water and 2 cups blueberries. Cook over medium heat until thickened and bubbly, stirring constantly. Cook for 2 minutes longer. Stir in lemon juice. Cool slightly. Serve with warm breakfast cake. May chill prepared breakfast cake overnight before baking.
Yield: 15 servings.

Approx Per Serving: Cal 339; Prot 6 g; Carbo 41 g; Fiber 2 g; T Fat 17 g; 46% Calories from Fat; Chol 47 mg; Sod 326 mg.

Karen Carney, Massachusetts

Brown Sugar Coffee Cake

1¹/₂ cups sifted flour
1 cup packed brown sugar
¹/₂ cup shortening
¹/₂ teaspoon baking powder
¹/₂ cup milk
1 egg, slightly beaten
1 teaspoon salt
1 teaspoon vanilla extract

Combine flour, brown sugar and shortening in bowl; mix until crumbly. Reserve ¹/₂ cup crumb mixture. Add baking powder, milk, egg, salt and vanilla to remaining crumb mixture in bowl; mix until moistened. Spoon into greased 8x11-inch baking pan. Top with reserved crumb mixture. Bake at 375 degrees for 10 minutes. Cool on wire rack for 20 minutes or longer. Serve warm or cool. Yield: 15 servings.

♥ **Approx Per Serving:** Cal 181; Prot 2 g; Carbo 27 g; Fiber <1 g; T Fat 8 g; 37% Calories from Fat; Chol 15 mg; Sod 169 mg.

Gail V. Bowlds, Massachusetts

Cinnamon-Chocolate Chip Coffee Cake

¹/₄ cup sugar
¹/₃ cup packed brown sugar
1³/₄ teaspoons cinnamon
1 cup chocolate chips
1 cup chopped walnuts
¹/₂ cup butter, softened
1 cup sugar
2 eggs
1 cup sour cream
2 teaspoons vanilla extract
2 cups sifted flour
1 teaspoon baking powder
1 teaspoon baking soda
Salt to taste

Combine ¹/₄ cup sugar, brown sugar, cinnamon, chocolate chips and walnuts in small bowl; mix well. Sprinkle ¹/₃ of the mixture into greased tube pan. Cream butter and 1 cup sugar in mixer bowl until light and fluffy. Beat in eggs, sour cream and vanilla. Mix flour, baking powder, baking soda and salt together. Add to batter; mix well. Layer batter and remaining walnut mixture ¹/₂ at a time in prepared tube pan. Bake at 350 degrees for 45 minutes. Cool in pan for several minutes. Remove to serving plate. Yield: 16 servings.

♥ **Approx Per Serving:** Cal 329; Prot 4 g; Carbo 40 g; Fiber 1 g; T Fat 18 g; 48% Calories from Fat; Chol 49 mg; Sod 142 mg.

Mary Jane Scholz, Massachusetts

Sour Cream Coffee Cake

1/2 cup shortening
3/4 cup sugar
2 eggs
1 teaspoon vanilla extract
2 cups flour
1 teaspoon baking powder
1 teaspoon baking soda
1 cup (generous) sour cream
1/4 cup sugar
1 teaspoon cinnamon
1/2 cup chopped walnuts
1 cup semisweet chocolate chips

Cream shortening and 3/4 cup sugar in mixer bowl until light and fluffy. Beat in eggs and vanilla. Mix flour, baking powder and baking soda together. Add to batter alternately with sour cream, mixing well after each addition and ending with sour cream. Mix 1/4 cup sugar and cinnamon in small bowl. Layer batter, cinnamon-sugar, walnuts and chocolate chips 1/2 at a time in greased 2-piece tube pan. Bake at 350 degrees for 35 to 45 minutes or just until tester comes out clean; do not overbake. Cool coffee cake in pan. Remove to serving plate. Yield: 16 servings.

Approx Per Serving: Cal 280; Prot 4 g; Carbo 32 g; Fiber 1 g; T Fat 16 g; 51% Calories from Fat; Chol 33 mg; Sod 91 mg.

Karen T. G. Tanzer, Massachusetts

Best-Ever Banana Bread

2 medium bananas, mashed
2 eggs
1/2 cup oil
5 tablespoons buttermilk
1 3/4 cups flour
1 1/2 cups sugar
1 teaspoon baking soda
1/2 teaspoon salt
1 teaspoon vanilla extract
1 cup chopped walnuts

Combine bananas, eggs, oil and buttermilk in bowl; mix well. Add flour, sugar, baking soda, salt and vanilla; mix well. Stir in walnuts. Spoon into greased and floured 5x9-inch loaf pan. Bake at 325 degrees for 1 hour and 20 minutes or until golden brown. May omit walnuts if preferred. Yield: 12 servings.

Approx Per Serving: Cal 340; Prot 5 g; Carbo 45 g; Fiber 1 g; T Fat 17 g; 43% Calories from Fat; Chol 36 mg; Sod 178 mg.

Anne Drinkwater and Jane Hughes, Massachusetts

Lila MacDonald's Vermont Banana Bread

This recipe was given to me 45 years ago by a good friend.
It came from her mother, a native Vermonter.

1 egg
1 cup sugar
1/3 cup shortening
3 very ripe bananas, mashed
2 cups flour
1 teaspoon baking powder
1 teaspoon baking soda
Salt to taste

*B*eat egg, sugar and shortening in mixer bowl until light. Beat in bananas. Sift in flour, baking powder, baking soda and salt. Spoon into greased loaf pan. Bake at 350 degrees for 45 minutes or until wooden pick comes out clean. Cool in pan for several minutes. Remove to wire rack to cool completely. Yield: 12 servings.

♥ **Approx Per Serving:** Cal 224; Prot 3 g; Carbo 39 g; Fiber 1 g; T Fat 7 g; 26% Calories from Fat; Chol 18 mg; Sod 103 mg.

Maizie S. Hescock, Vermont

Calzone

1 cup sliced mushrooms
1/2 cup chopped green bell pepper
1 tablespoon margarine
1 pound frozen bread dough, thawed
1   10-ounce package frozen chopped broccoli, cooked, drained
4 ounces thinly sliced ham
4 ounces thinly sliced hard salami
4 ounces thinly sliced provolone cheese
1 1/2 ounces thinly sliced pepperoni

*S*auté mushrooms and green pepper in margarine in large skillet for 2 to 3 minutes or until tender; remove from heat. Press dough into 8x14-inch rectangle on baking sheet lined with lightly greased foil. Layer broccoli, ham, salami, cheese and pepperoni down center of dough. Top with mushroom and pepper mixture. Make 6 to 8 slices from each long edge to within 1 inch of filling. Fold strips alternately over filling. Let rise, covered, for 1 to 1 1/2 hours or until doubled in bulk. Bake at 350 degrees for 45 minutes or until brown. Yield: 8 servings.

♥ **Approx Per Serving:** Cal 302; Prot 16 g; Carbo 34 g; Fiber 1 g; T Fat 13 g; 38% Calories from Fat; Chol 29 mg; Sod 941 mg.

Donna Spencer, Massachusetts

Cranberry Bread

2 cups flour
1 cup sugar
1¹/₂ teaspoons baking powder
¹/₂ teaspoon baking soda
1 teaspoon salt
³/₄ cup orange juice
Grated rind of 1 orange
1 egg, beaten
2 tablespoons melted butter
1¹/₂ cups cranberry halves
¹/₂ cup walnuts

Sift flour, sugar, baking powder, baking soda and salt into large bowl. Add orange juice, orange rind, egg and butter; mix well. Stir in cranberries and walnuts. Spoon into greased and floured loaf pan. Let stand for 20 minutes. Bake at 325 degrees for 1 hour. Cool in pan for several minutes. Remove to wire rack to cool completely. Yield: 12 servings.

♥ **Approx Per Serving:** Cal 210; Prot 4 g; Carbo 37 g; Fiber 1 g; T Fat 6 g; 24% Calories from Fat; Chol 23 mg; Sod 276 mg.

Celeste Buckley, Massachusetts

Date and Nut Bread

I have had this recipe since I was a bride 50 years ago. Each year I make dozens of these loaves for Christmas gifts.

1 cup boiling water
2 cups chopped dates
1 cup broken walnuts
¹/₄ cup shortening
³/₄ cup packed brown sugar
1 egg
1 teaspoon baking soda
2 cups flour
¹/₂ teaspoon salt
¹/₃ cup cold water

Pour boiling water over dates and walnuts in bowl. Let stand for several minutes. Cream shortening and brown sugar in mixer bowl until light and fluffy. Beat in egg. Stir baking soda into date mixture. Add to creamed mixture alternately with flour and salt, mixing well after each addition. Stir in ¹/₃ cup cold water. Spoon into greased 5x9-inch loaf pan. Bake at 350 degrees for 55 to 60 minutes or until tester comes out clean. Cool in pan for several minutes. Remove to wire rack to cool completely. Yield: 12 servings.

♥ **Approx Per Serving:** Cal 330; Prot 5 g; Carbo 56 g; Fiber 4 g; T Fat 11 g; 29% Calories from Fat; Chol 18 mg; Sod 173 mg.

Martha Baer, New Jersey

English Muffin Bread

5¹/₂ to 6 cups flour
2 envelopes dry yeast
1 tablespoon sugar
¹/₄ teaspoon baking soda
2 teaspoons salt
2 cups skim milk
¹/₂ cup water

Combine 3 cups flour, yeast, sugar, baking soda and salt in bowl. Heat milk and water in saucepan until very warm. Add to dry ingredients; mix well. Stir in enough additional flour to make a stiff batter. Spoon into two 5x9-inch loaf pans which have been greased and sprinkled with cornmeal. Let rise, covered, for 45 minutes. Bake at 400 degrees for 25 minutes. Remove immediately to wire rack to cool. Slice and toast to serve. Yield: 24 servings.

Approx Per Serving: Cal 125; Prot 4 g; Carbo 26 g; Fiber 1 g; T Fat <1 g; 3% Calories from Fat; Chol <1 mg; Sod 198 mg.

Mary T. McGinnis, Florida

Holiday Gift Loaves

1 cup butter, softened
8 ounces cream cheese, softened
1 cup sugar
1¹/₂ teaspoons vanilla extract
4 eggs
1¹/₂ teaspoons baking powder
2¹/₄ cups flour
³/₄ cup drained chopped
  maraschino cherries
¹/₂ cup chopped pecans

Cream butter, cream cheese, sugar and vanilla in mixer bowl until light and fluffy. Beat in eggs 1 at a time. Add baking powder and 2 cups flour; mix well. Toss remaining ¹/₄ cup flour with cherries and pecans in bowl. Fold into batter. Spoon into greased 4x8-inch loaf pans. Bake at 325 degrees for 1 hour. Cool in pans. Yield: 24 servings.

Approx Per Serving: Cal 214; Prot 3 g; Carbo 20 g; Fiber 1 g; T Fat 14 g; 57% Calories from Fat; Chol 67 mg; Sod 125 mg.

Donna Takacs, Massachusetts

Nellie O'Leary's Irish Soda Bread

This recipe is attributed to Nellie T. O'Donoghue O'Leary who arrived at Ellis Island in 1920 from the Irish village of Rathmore. Legend has it that the immigrants from her village subsisted largely on Nellie's soda bread during the crossing from the Emerald Isle.

4 cups flour
1 cup sugar
4 teaspoons baking powder
1/2 teaspoon salt
1/2 cup melted butter
1 1/2 cups raisins
2 tablespoons caraway seed
1 1/2 cups buttermilk
1 egg, slightly beaten
1/3 teaspoon baking soda
1 teaspoon melted butter

Sift first 4 ingredients into bowl. Add 1/2 cup butter; mix well. Stir in raisins and caraway seed; make well in center. Add mixture of buttermilk, egg and baking soda; mix well. Spoon into greased large cast-iron skillet. Make cross in top with knife; brush cross with 1 teaspoon melted butter. Bake at 375 degrees for 1 hour or until golden brown. Yield: 16 servings.

♥ **Approx Per Serving:** Cal 279; Prot 5 g; Carbo 50 g; Fiber 2 g; T Fat 7 g; 22% Calories from Fat; Chol 30 mg; Sod 256 mg.

Brenda Reilly, Massachusetts

Lemon Bread

1/2 cup butter, softened
1 cup sugar
2 eggs
Juice of 1 lemon
1 1/2 cups flour
1 teaspoon baking powder
1/2 cup milk
1 cup sugar
Juice and grated rind of 1 lemon

Cream butter and 1 cup sugar in mixer bowl until light and fluffy. Beat in eggs and juice of 1 lemon. Sift flour and baking powder together. Add to batter alternately with milk, mixing well after each addition. Spoon into greased loaf pan. Bake at 375 degrees for 45 minutes. Pierce holes in loaf with fork. Boil 1 cup sugar with juice and grated rind of 1 lemon in saucepan. Drizzle over bread. Cool in pan. Yield: 12 servings.

♥ **Approx Per Serving:** Cal 275; Prot 3 g; Carbo 47 g; Fiber <1 g; T Fat 9 g; 29% Calories from Fat; Chol 58 mg; Sod 109 mg.

Barbara Porter, Massachusetts

Oatmeal Bread

2 cups boiling water
1 cup oats
1 envelope dry yeast or 1 cake yeast
1/2 cup warm water
1/2 cup molasses
1 tablespoon butter
2 teaspoons salt
5 cups flour

Pour boiling water over oats in bowl. Let stand for 1 hour. Dissolve yeast in warm water in small bowl. Add molasses, butter, salt, yeast and flour to oats; mix well. Let rise until nearly doubled in bulk. Stir batter down. Let rise again. Spoon into 2 greased loaf pans. Bake at 375 degrees for 40 to 60 minutes or until golden brown. May shape into biscuits and bake at 400 to 425 degrees until brown if preferred.
Yield: 24 servings.

♥ **Approx Per Serving:** Cal 127; Prot 3 g; Carbo 26 g; Fiber 1 g; T Fat 1 g; 7% Calories from Fat; Chol 1 mg; Sod 183 mg.

Glenn B. Knight, Ph.D., Massachusetts

Oatmeal and Molasses Bread

1 cup sifted all-purpose flour
1 cup sifted rye flour
1 teaspoon baking powder
1 teaspoon baking soda
1 teaspoon salt
1 cup oats
1/4 cup sugar
1/2 cup molasses
1 1/4 cups buttermilk
1 cup raisins
1/2 cup chopped walnuts

Sift all-purpose flour and rye flour into bowl. Add baking powder, baking soda, salt, oats and sugar; mix well. Add molasses and buttermilk gradually, mixing until smooth. Stir in raisins and walnuts. Spoon into greased 5x9-inch loaf pan. Let stand for 20 minutes. Bake at 350 degrees for 1 hour. Cool in pan.
Yield: 12 servings.

♥ **Approx Per Serving:** Cal 220; Prot 5 g; Carbo 43 g; Fiber 3 g; T Fat 4 g; 16% Calories from Fat; Chol 1 mg; Sod 305 mg.

Margaret Satterly, New York

Autumn Pumpkin Loaves

3 cups sugar
1 cup oil
4 eggs
3½ cups flour
2 teaspoons baking soda
1 teaspoon cinnamon
1 teaspoon nutmeg
1½ teaspoons salt
⅔ cup cold water
2 cups pumpkin
1 cup chopped walnuts
1 cup raisins

Combine sugar and oil in mixer bowl; beat until smooth. Beat in eggs 1 at a time. Mix flour, baking soda, cinnamon, nutmeg and salt together. Add to egg mixture alternately with water and pumpkin. Fold in walnuts and raisins. Spoon into 3 greased small loaf pans, filling ½ full. Bake at 350 degrees for 1 hour. Cool in pans for several minutes. Remove to wire rack to cool completely. Yield: 18 servings.

♥ **Approx Per Serving:** Cal 421; Prot 5 g; Carbo 63 g; Fiber 2 g; T Fat 18 g; 37% Calories from Fat; Chol 47 mg; Sod 289 mg.

Patricia A. Newton, Massachusetts

Zucchini Bread

2 cups sugar
4 eggs
1½ cups oil
1 tablespoon vanilla extract
2 teaspoons cinnamon
1½ teaspoons salt
1½ teaspoons baking soda
1½ teaspoons baking powder
4½ cups flour
3 cups shredded zucchini

Combine sugar, eggs, oil and vanilla in mixer bowl; beat until smooth. Add cinnamon, salt, baking soda, baking powder and flour in order listed, mixing until smooth after each addition. Stir in zucchini. Spoon into 3 greased and floured 5x9-inch loaf pans. Bake at 350 degrees for 1 hour. Cool in pans for several minutes. Remove to wire rack to cool completely. May add raisins, nuts or drained 20-ounce can of crushed pineapple if desired. Yield: 36 servings.

♥ **Approx Per Serving:** Cal 193; Prot 3 g; Carbo 24 g; Fiber 1 g; T Fat 10 g; 46% Calories from Fat; Chol 24 mg; Sod 146 mg.

Genevieve V. Kacmarczyk, Massachusetts

Whole Wheat-Walnut Bread

¹/₄ cup sugar
1 envelope dry yeast
2¹/₂ cups warm water
5 cups all-purpose flour
4 cups whole wheat flour
1 tablespoon (scant) salt
¹/₄ cup melted butter
2 cups broken walnuts
1 egg, beaten

Dissolve sugar and yeast in water. Mix with flours and salt in bowl. Add butter; mix to form dough. Knead on floured surface for 10 minutes or until smooth and elastic. Place in greased bowl, turning to coat surface. Let rise, covered, for 60 minutes or until doubled in bulk. Roll into three 6x8-inch rectangles on floured surface. Spinkle with walnuts. Roll up, stretching as you roll; seal edges. Place seam side down on baking sheet sprinkled with cornmeal. Let rise, covered, for 30 minutes or until doubled in bulk. Cut 3 slashes on top of each. Brush with egg. Bake at 350 degrees for 30 minutes or until golden brown. Cool on wire rack. Yield: 36 servings.

♥ **Approx Per Serving:** Cal 170; Prot 5 g; Carbo 25 g; Fiber 3 g; T Fat 6 g; 31% Calories from Fat; Chol 9 mg; Sod 192 mg.

Christine B. Thomas, M.D., Massachusetts

Bran Muffins

2 cups 100% bran cereal
¹/₂ cup oil
1 cup each raisins and boiling water
2 eggs
2 cups milk
¹/₄ cup molasses
2¹/₄ cups whole wheat flour
¹/₄ cup packed brown sugar
2¹/₂ teaspoons baking soda
¹/₂ teaspoon salt

Combine cereal, oil, raisins and boiling water in large bowl; mix well. Beat eggs, milk and molasses in small bowl. Add to cereal mixture; mix well. Mix flour, brown sugar, baking soda and salt together. Add to batter; stir until moistened. Spoon into greased muffin cups. Bake at 350 degrees for 25 minutes. Yield: 24 servings.

♥ **Approx Per Serving:** Cal 150; Prot 4 g; Carbo 23 g; Fiber 3 g; T Fat 6 g; 34% Calories from Fat; Chol 21 mg; Sod 185 mg.

Betty Hunt, Massachusetts

Morning Glory Muffins

2 cups flour or 1¹/₃ cups flour and
  ²/₃ cup oat bran
³/₄ cup sugar
2 teaspoons baking soda
2 teaspoons cinnamon
1 8-ounce can crushed pineapple
2 tablespoons oil
¹/₂ cup (or more) orange juice
3 eggs, beaten or ³/₄ cup egg
  substitute
1 apple, grated or chopped
1¹/₂ cups grated carrots
¹/₄ cup chopped walnuts

Sift first 4 ingredients together. Drain pineapple, reserving juice. Combine reserved juice with oil and enough orange juice to measure 1 cup. Combine juice mixture with eggs in large bowl; whisk until smooth. Add remaining ingredients and flour mixture; mix just until moistened. Spoon into muffin cups sprayed with nonstick cooking spray. Bake at 400 degrees for 18 minutes or until golden. Yield: 18 servings.

💜 **Approx Per Serving:** Cal 145; Prot 3 g; Carbo 26 g; Fiber 1 g;
  T Fat 4 g; 23% Calories from Fat; Chol 36 mg; Sod 107 mg.

Rebecca Bradley, M.S., R.D., Massachusetts

Filled Buns

1¹/₂ pounds ground beef
2 tablespoons chopped onion
1¹/₂ cups drained canned mixed
  vegetables
¹/₂ 10-ounce can cream of
  mushroom soup
2 tablespoons soy sauce
Salt and pepper to taste
3 1-pound loaves frozen bread
  dough, thawed
2 tablespoons melted butter

Brown ground beef with onion in skillet, stirring frequently; drain. Stir in next 3 ingredients. Cook for 5 minutes. Add salt and pepper. Chill until needed. Cut dough into 21 slices. Press into 4¹/₂-inch circles on floured surface. Spoon chilled mixture onto circles. Twist edges of dough to enclose filling. Place seam side down on greased baking sheets. Let rise for 30 minutes. Bake at 375 to 400 degrees for 20 minutes. Brush with butter. Cool on wire rack. Store in refrigerator. Yield: 21 servings.

💜 **Approx Per Serving:** Cal 251; Prot 11 g; Carbo 37 g; Fiber <1 g;
  T Fat 9 g; 29% Calories from Fat; Chol 24 mg; Sod 591 mg.

Ruth Fillmore, Minnesota

Desserts

Apple Bavarian Torte

1 cup flour
1/3 cup sugar
1/2 teaspoon vanilla extract
1/2 cup butter
16 ounces cream cheese, softened
1/2 cup sugar
1 teaspoon vanilla extract
2 eggs, at room temperature
1/4 cup sugar
1/2 teaspoon cinnamon
1/2 teaspoon vanilla extract
2 large tart green apples, peeled,
    thinly sliced
1/3 cup coarsely chopped walnuts

Combine flour, 1/3 cup sugar and 1/2 teaspoon vanilla in bowl; mix well. Cut in 1/2 cup butter until crumbly. Press onto bottom and up side of 10-inch springform pan. Bake at 450 degrees for 5 minutes or until golden brown. Beat cream cheese, 1/2 cup sugar and 1 teaspoon vanilla in mixer bowl until smooth. Beat in eggs 1 at a time. Spoon into baked crust. Combine 1/4 cup sugar, cinnamon and 1/2 teaspoon vanilla in bowl; mix well. Add apple slices, tossing to coat apples with mixture. Spoon over cream cheese layer. Sprinkle with walnuts. Bake at 450 degrees for 15 minutes. Reduce oven temperature to 350 degrees. Bake for 45 minutes longer or until apples are tender. Cool in pan on rack. Remove sides of springform pan. Chill in refrigerator. Let stand at room temperature for 30 minutes before serving. Yield: 6 servings.

♥ **Approx Per Serving:** Cal 712; Prot 11 g; Carbo 62 g; Fiber 2 g; T Fat 48 g; 60% Calories from Fat; Chol 195 mg; Sod 378 mg.

Kathryn Burke, Massachusetts

Sharon Cohen, M.S., P.T., with young patients at the Bedford Orthopaedic Hospital in Umtata, South Africa

Apple Torte

1 cup sugar
1/2 cup butter
1 cup sifted flour
1 teaspoon baking powder
1/4 teaspoon salt
2 eggs
3 apples, peeled, sliced
2 teaspoons sugar
2 tablespoons cinnamon
1/2 teaspoon lemon juice

Cream sugar and butter in mixer bowl until light and fluffy. Add flour, baking powder and salt; mix well. Beat in eggs 1 at a time. Pour into greased 9-inch springform pan. Spread apple slices over top clockwise around edge and counterclockwise around center. Sprinkle with mixture of 2 teaspoons sugar and cinnamon. Sprinkle with lemon juice. Bake at 350 degrees for 1 hour. Serve warm with whipped cream or cold. Yield: 6 servings.

Approx Per Serving: Cal 402; Prot 4 g; Carbo 59 g; Fiber 2 g; T Fat 18 g; 38% Calories from Fat; Chol 112 mg; Sod 297 mg.

Nancy Nichols, Massachusetts

Blueberry Buckle

3/4 cup sugar
1/4 cup shortening
1 egg
1/2 cup milk
2 cups flour
2 teaspoons baking powder
1/2 teaspoon salt
2 cups thawed frozen blueberries
1/2 cup sugar
1/2 cup flour
1/2 teaspoon cinnamon
1/4 cup margarine, softened

Cream 3/4 cup sugar and shortening in mixer bowl until light and fluffy. Beat in egg. Add milk; mix well. Mix 2 cups flour, baking powder and salt together. Add to mixture; mix well. Fold in blueberries. Spread batter in greased and floured 7x14-inch baking dish. Combine remaining 1/2 cup sugar, 1/2 cup flour and cinnamon in bowl. Cut in margarine until crumbly. Sprinkle over batter. Bake at 375 degrees for 45 minutes. Yield: 15 servings.

Approx Per Serving: Cal 219; Prot 3 g; Carbo 36 g; Fiber 1 g; T Fat 7 g; 30% Calories from Fat; Chol 15 mg; Sod 160 mg.

Marie G. McDonough, Massachusetts

Chilled Chocolate Tortoni

8 ounces semisweet chocolate,
  broken
2/3 cup light corn syrup
2 cups whipping cream
1 1/2 cups chocolate wafer cookie
  crumbs
1 cup chopped walnuts

Combine chocolate and corn syrup in saucepan. Heat over low heat until chocolate is melted, stirring frequently. Stir in 1/2 cup cream. Remove from heat. Chill in refrigerator. Beat remaining 1 1/2 cups cream in mixer bowl until soft peaks form. Fold in chilled chocolate mixture, cookie crumbs and walnuts. Spoon into small paper muffin cup liners. Freeze, covered, for 4 to 6 hours or until firm. Let stand at room temperature for several minutes before serving. Garnish with additional melted chocolate or walnuts. May substitute 8 ounces whipped topping for cream.
Yield: 24 servings.

♥ **Approx Per Serving:** Cal 217; Prot 2 g; Carbo 21 g; Fiber <1 g;
T Fat 15 g; 59% Calories from Fat; Chol 27 mg; Sod 82 mg.

Fran McNeeley, Massachusetts

Cream Cheese Torte

19 ounces cream cheese, softened
1 cup sugar
3/4 teaspoon vanilla extract
2 cups whipping cream, whipped
2 12-count packages plain
  ladyfingers
1 21-ounce can cherry pie filling

Combine cream cheese, sugar and vanilla in bowl; mix well. Fold in whipped cream. Line bottom and side of greased 9-inch springform pan with ladyfingers. Pour in cream cheese mixture. Top with cherry pie filling. Chill in refrigerator overnight. Remove side of springform pan.
Yield: 10 servings.

♥ **Approx Per Serving:** Cal 581; Prot 7 g; Carbo 55 g; Fiber 1 g;
T Fat 38 g; 58% Calories from Fat; Chol 218 mg; Sod 225 mg.

Ellen Byda, Massachusetts

Chocolate Ladyfinger Dream

2 ounces German's sweet chocolate
2¹/₂ tablespoons confectioners' sugar
3 tablespoons water
¹/₈ teaspoon salt
4 egg yolks, beaten
4 egg whites, stiffly beaten
16 ladyfingers, cut into halves
1 cup whipping cream, whipped

Line 2-quart dish with waxed paper, allowing 2-inch collar around top. Melt chocolate with confectioners' sugar, water and salt in top of double boiler, stirring frequently. Stir in egg yolks. Remove from heat. Fold in stiffly beaten egg whites. Alternate layers of ladyfingers and chocolate mixture in prepared dish, reversing ladyfingers direction on each layer. Chill in refrigerator overnight. Unmold onto serving dish; remove waxed paper. Serve sliced with whipped cream. Yield: 6 servings.

♥ **Approx Per Serving:** Cal 354; Prot 8 g; Carbo 29 g; Fiber <1 g; T Fat 24 g; 59% Calories from Fat; Chol 301 mg; Sod 132 mg.

Alice G. Davis, Maine

Creamy Baked Cheesecake

¹/₃ cup melted margarine
1¹/₄ cups graham cracker crumbs
¹/₄ cup sugar
16 ounces cream cheese, softened
1   14-ounce can sweetened condensed milk
3 eggs
¹/₄ cup lemon juice concentrate
1 cup sour cream

Combine margarine, graham cracker crumbs and sugar in bowl; mix well. Press onto bottom of greased 9-inch springform pan. Beat cream cheese and condensed milk in mixer bowl until smooth. Add eggs and lemon juice concentrate; mix well. Pour into prepared pan. Bake at 300 degrees for 50 to 55 minutes or until set. Top with sour cream. Bake for 5 minutes longer. Chill until serving time. May add favorite topping. Yield: 8 servings.

♥ **Approx Per Serving:** Cal 622; Prot 13 g; Carbo 51 g; Fiber <1 g; T Fat 42 g; 60% Calories from Fat; Chol 192 mg; Sod 453 mg.

Joanne Duncan, Massachusetts

Quick Fruit Crisp

The Swinton family has made this recipe all over the world using local fruit. It is universally loved for its fruit flavor and American ease.

2 cups blueberries
1 cup flour
1 cup sugar
1 teaspoon baking powder
1/2 teaspoon salt
1 egg
1 teaspoon vanilla extract
1/2 cup melted butter

Spread blueberries in buttered 9-inch-deep baking dish. Combine flour, sugar, baking powder and salt in bowl; mix well. Add egg and vanilla; mix well. Sprinkle over blueberries; drizzle butter over top. Bake at 375 degrees for 35 minutes. Serve immediately with ice cream. May substitute 2 cups blackberries or raspberries or 3 cups sliced apples, pears or peaches for blueberries. May marinate pears in rum for 20 minutes and substitute almond extract for vanilla.
Yield: 6 servings.

♥ **Approx Per Serving:** Cal 383; Prot 4 g; Carbo 56 g; Fiber 2 g;
T Fat 17 g; 38% Calories from Fat; Chol 77 mg; Sod 377 mg.

Neil and Elizabeth Swinton, Massachusetts

Chocolate Mousse

8 ounces semisweet chocolate
8 egg yolks, beaten
2 tablespoons Grand Marnier
1/2 cup sugar
8 egg whites, stiffly beaten

Melt chocolate in double boiler over hot water. Cool. Combine egg yolks and Grand Marnier in bowl; mix well. Add sugar to chocolate; mix well. Add egg yolks mixture; mix well. Fold in stiffly beaten egg whites. Chill, covered, in refrigerator for 2 hours. Spoon into serving dishes.
Yield: 8 servings.

♥ **Approx Per Serving:** Cal 271; Prot 8 g; Carbo 31 g; Fiber 0 g;
T Fat 15 g; 46% Calories from Fat; Chol 213 mg; Sod 59 mg.

Sue Landry, Massachusetts

Lime Mousse

This is the perfect light dessert after a heavy meal.

1/2 cup unsalted butter
5 eggs
1 cup sugar
3/4 cup fresh lime juice
Grated rind of 5 limes
2 cups whipping cream, chilled

Melt butter in double boiler over simmering water. Beat eggs and sugar in mixer bowl until light and foamy. Add to butter. Cook for 8 minutes or until mixture thickens, stirring constantly. Remove from heat. Stir in lime juice and grated rind. Cool to room temperature. Beat cream in mixer bowl until very stiff, almost to the point of becoming butter. Stir lime mixture into whipped cream. Chill for 4 hours. Yield: 8 servings.

♥ **Approx Per Serving:** Cal 460; Prot 5 g; Carbo 30 g; Fiber <1 g; T Fat 37 g; 70% Calories from Fat; Chol 246 mg; Sod 163 mg.

Nancy Makarowski, Massachusetts

Pear Streusel

I have been making this for over 25 years. I double bagged the vanilla wafers and my children assisted by jumping on them to make cookie crumbs.

2 29-ounce cans pear halves, drained
1 10 or 12-ounce package vanilla wafers, crushed
2 tablespoons sugar
1/2 cup melted butter

Place pears in buttered 10-inch baking dish. Combine vanilla wafer crumbs, sugar and butter in bowl; mix well. Sprinkle over pears. Bake at 300 degrees for 20 minutes. Serve warm, not hot, with ice cream. May layer streusel and ice cream in parfait glasses. Yield: 8 servings.

♥ **Approx Per Serving:** Cal 427; Prot 3 g; Carbo 65 g; Fiber 3 g; T Fat 19 g; 39% Calories from Fat; Chol 58 mg; Sod 267 mg.

Leigh Smith, R.N., Massachusetts

Pistachio Dessert

3/4 cup margarine
1 1/2 cups flour
1/2 cup chopped walnuts
8 ounces cream cheese, softened
1 cup confectioners' sugar
16 ounces whipped topping
2 3-ounce packages pistachio
  instant pudding mix
1 1/2 cups milk

Cut margarine into flour in bowl until crumbly. Stir in walnuts. Press onto bottom of buttered 9x13-inch baking dish. Bake at 375 degrees for 15 to 20 minutes or until brown. Combine cream cheese and confectioners' sugar in mixer bowl; beat well. Fold in 1/2 of the whipped topping. Spread over baked crust. Beat pudding mix and milk in mixer bowl until smooth. Spread over cream cheese layer; top with remaining whipped topping. Garnish with additional walnuts and maraschino cherries. Chill in refrigerator for 3 hours to overnight. Yield: 24 servings.

♥ **Approx Per Serving:** Cal 243; Prot 3 g; Carbo 23 g; Fiber <1 g;
T Fat 16 g; 58% Calories from Fat; Chol 12 mg; Sod 154 mg.

Priscille St. Louis, Massachusetts

Fruit Pizza

1 20-ounce roll refrigerator sugar
  cookie dough
1/3 cup cream cheese, softened
1/3 cup sugar
1/2 teaspoon vanilla extract
1/2 cup strawberries
1/2 cup blueberries
1/2 cup sliced kiwifruit
1/2 cup sliced bananas
1/2 cup sliced peaches
1/4 cup orange marmalade
1 tablespoon water

Slice cookie dough. Spread cookie slices on greased and floured baking pan, pressing edges together. Bake at 375 degrees for 15 to 20 minutes or until brown. Cool. Combine cream cheese, sugar and vanilla in bowl; mix well. Spread on cooled layer. Arrange fruit over top. Mix marmalade and 1 tablespoon water in bowl. Spread over fruit. May substitute your favorite fruit. Yield: 10 servings.

♥ **Approx Per Serving:** Cal 420; Prot 6 g; Carbo 475 g; Fiber 1 g;
T Fat 17 g; 7% Calories from Fat; Chol 9 mg; Sod 346 mg.

Mary Gifford, New Hampshire

Bread Pudding

1/4 cup butter, softened
4 slices white bread, crusts trimmed
1 cup packed brown sugar
2 eggs, beaten
2 cups milk
1/8 teaspoon salt
1 teaspoon vanilla extract

Spread butter on bread slices; cut into cubes. Layer brown sugar and bread cubes in top of double boiler. Combine eggs, milk, salt and vanilla in bowl; mix well. Pour over layers. Do not stir. Steam, covered, over hot water for 1½ hours. Yield: 6 servings.

♥ **Approx Per Serving:** Cal 352; Prot 6 g; Carbo 55 g; Fiber <1 g; T Fat 13 g; 32% Calories from Fat; Chol 103 mg; Sod 253 mg.

Nancy Braasch, Massachusetts

Grape Nut Pudding

1 cup Grape Nuts
1 quart milk
3 eggs, beaten
1 cup sugar
1 teaspoon vanilla extract
Salt to taste

Combine Grape Nuts and milk in double boiler. Cook over hot water for 20 minutes. Add eggs, sugar, vanilla and salt; mix well. Pour into buttered baking dish. Bake at 350 degrees for 50 minutes or until set. Garnish with whipped cream. Yield: 6 servings.

♥ **Approx Per Serving:** Cal 338; Prot 11 g; Carbo 57 g; Fiber 1 g; T Fat 8 g; 22% Calories from Fat; Chol 128 mg; Sod 235 mg.

Mary Richards, New Hampshire

Lemon Sponge Pudding

1 cup sugar
1 1/2 tablespoons flour
1/4 cup melted butter
1 cup milk
2 egg yolks, beaten
Juice and grated rind of 1 lemon
2 egg whites, stiffly beaten

Combine sugar, flour and butter in bowl; mix well. Add milk, egg yolks, lemon juice and rind; mix well. Fold in egg whites gently. Pour into buttered baking dish. Place dish in baking pan half filled with hot water. Bake at 350 degrees for 45 minutes. Yield: 8 servings.

♥ **Approx Per Serving:** Cal 193; Prot 3 g; Carbo 28 g; Fiber <1 g; T Fat 8 g; 37% Calories from Fat; Chol 73 mg; Sod 76 mg.

Doris E. Ludlam, Pennsylvania

Noodle Pudding

12 ounces medium noodles, cooked
1/2 cup melted margarine
1/2 cup orange juice
1/2 cup sugar
4 eggs
1/2 cup seedless raisins
1/2 cup golden seedless raisins
1/2 teaspoon salt
1 21-ounce can apple pie filling
1/2 cup crushed cornflakes
3 tablespoons sugar
1/2 teaspoon cinnamon
Juice of 1/2 lemon

Combine noodles, margarine, orange juice, 1/2 cup sugar and eggs in large bowl; mix well. Stir in raisins, salt and pie filling. Pour into buttered 9x13-inch baking dish. Mix cornflakes, 3 tablespoons sugar, cinnamon and lemon juice in bowl. Sprinkle over pudding. Bake at 350 degrees for 1 hour. Yield: 15 servings.

♥ **Approx Per Serving:** Cal 282; Prot 6 g; Carbo 47 g; Fiber 1 g; T Fat 9 g; 27% Calories from Fat; Chol 97 mg; Sod 206 mg.

Richard V. Abdo, M.D., Massachusetts

Mrs. Truman's Ozark Pudding

2 eggs, beaten
1¹/₂ cups sugar
4¹/₂ tablespoons flour
2¹/₂ teaspoons baking powder
¹/₈ teaspoon salt
1¹/₂ teaspoons vanilla extract
³/₄ cup chopped pecans
1 cup chopped apple
1 cup whipped cream

Combine eggs and sugar in mixer bowl; beat until light. Sift flour, baking powder and salt together. Add to eggs; mix well. Fold in vanilla, pecans and apple. Pour into greased 2-quart casserole. Bake at 325 degrees for 30 minutes. Serve with whipped cream. Yield: 6 servings.

♥ **Approx Per Serving:** Cal 494; Prot 5 g; Carbo 62 g; Fiber 2 g; T Fat 27 g; 47% Calories from Fat; Chol 125 mg; Sod 221 mg.

Beth Landry, Massachusetts

Portuguese Rice Pudding

5 cups milk
³/₄ cup sugar
1 cup uncooked rice
¹/₂ teaspoon salt
4 eggs, beaten
Cinnamon to taste

Combine milk, sugar, rice and salt in double boiler. Cook over hot water until rice is tender, stirring occasionally. Stir a small amount of hot rice into eggs. Stir eggs into hot rice. Cook until thickened, stirring frequently. Spoon into serving dishes; sprinkle with cinnamon. Cool before serving. Yield: 4 servings.

♥ **Approx Per Serving:** Cal 578; Prot 19 g; Carbo 89 g; Fiber 1 g; T Fat 16 g; 25% Calories from Fat; Chol 254 mg; Sod 466 mg.

J. Philip Teixeira, Massachusetts

Lorry's Swedish Pudding

2 cups water
3/4 cup packed brown sugar
2 tablespoons butter
3/4 cup sugar
1 cup flour
2 teaspoons baking powder
1/2 teaspoon salt
1/2 cup milk
1 cup chopped dates

Bring water to a boil in saucepan. Add brown sugar and butter. Cook for 2 minutes, stirring constantly. Cool. Sift sugar, flour, baking powder and salt together into bowl. Add milk; mix well. Stir in dates. Add to brown sugar mixture; mix well. Spoon into buttered baking dish. Bake at 325 degrees for 40 minutes. Garnish with whipped cream. Yield: 4 servings.

♥ **Approx Per Serving:** Cal 645; Prot 5 g; Carbo 145 g; Fiber 4 g;
T Fat 7 g; 10% Calories from Fat; Chol 20 mg; Sod 518 mg.

Lois Shand, Massachusetts

Banana Sorbet

3 overripe bananas, frozen
Several drops of water
Artificial sweetener to taste

Cut ends from bananas; discard. Cut bananas into halves crosswise. Peel carefully, preserving as much fruit as possible. Cut bananas into chunks; place in blender or food processor container. Process until fruit is puréed and creamy, adding water and artificial sweetener to taste. Spoon into serving dishes. May also flavor with confectioners' sugar, orange liqueur, rum or instant pudding mix. Freeze bananas in skins when they become overripe.
Yield: 4 servings.

♥ **Approx Per Serving:** Cal 79; Prot 1 g; Carbo 20 g; Fiber 2 g;
T Fat <1 g; 4% Calories from Fat; Chol 0 mg; Sod 1 mg.

Grace M. Sargent, New Hampshire

Chocolate Stack Cake

1 cup margarine
2 cups flour
1/2 to 3/4 cup chopped pecans
8 ounces whipped topping
8 ounces cream cheese, softened
1 3/4 cups confectioners' sugar
1   4-ounce package chocolate
   instant pudding mix
1   4-ounce package vanilla instant
   pudding mix
3 cups milk
8 ounces whipped topping

Mix margarine, flour and pecans in bowl. Pat into 9x13-inch baking pan. Bake at 350 degrees for 25 minutes. Mix 8 ounces whipped topping, cream cheese and confectioners' sugar in bowl. Spread over cooled crust. Combine pudding mixes and milk in bowl; mix well. Spread over cream cheese mixture. Spread with remaining 8 ounces whipped topping. Chill until serving time. Yield: 15 servings.

♥ **Approx Per Serving:** Cal 498; Prot 5 g; Carbo 52 g; Fiber 1 g;
  T Fat 31 g; 55% Calories from Fat; Chol 23 mg; Sod 317 mg.

Betsy Plummer, Massachusetts

Moon Cake

After baking, this cake will look like the moon's surface.

1 cup water
1/2 cup butter
1 cup flour
4 eggs
2   4-ounce packages vanilla instant
   pudding mix
8 ounces cream cheese, softened
1 cup whipping cream, whipped
1   8-ounce can chocolate sauce
1 cup chopped pecans

Mix water and butter in saucepan. Bring to a boil. Stir in flour rapidly until mixture forms a ball. Remove from heat. Let stand until cool. Beat in eggs 1 at a time. Spread on ungreased baking sheet. Bake at 400 degrees for 30 minutes. Prepare pudding mix using package directions. Beat in cream cheese. Spread over cooled crust. Chill for 20 minutes. Spread with whipped cream. Drizzle with sauce. Sprinkle with pecans. Yield: 20 servings.

♥ **Approx Per Serving:** Cal 328; Prot 6 g; Carbo 29 g; Fiber 1 g;
  T Fat 22 g; 59% Calories from Fat; Chol 93 mg; Sod 328 mg.

Helen Drover, Massachusetts

Fresh Apple Cake

3 cups sifted flour
1 teaspoon baking soda
1/2 teaspoon salt
11/2 cups oil
2 cups sugar
3 eggs
2 teaspoons vanilla extract
1 cup chopped pecans
3 cups chopped peeled apples
1 cup packed dark brown sugar
1/2 cup margarine
1/4 cup milk

Sift flour, baking soda and salt together. Combine oil, sugar, eggs and vanilla in bowl; mix well. Stir in flour mixture. Fold in pecans and apples. Pour into greased tube pan. Bake at 350 degrees for 1 hour. Mix brown sugar, margarine and milk in saucepan. Bring to a boil. Simmer for 1 minute. Pour over hot cake. Cool in pan for 2 hours. Invert onto serving plate. Yield: 16 servings.

Approx Per Serving: Cal 552; Prot 4 g; Carbo 63 g; Fiber 2 g;
T Fat 33 g; 52% Calories from Fat; Chol 41 mg; Sod 208 mg.

Beverley Guerard, Massachusetts

Black Bottom Cupcakes

11/2 cups flour
1 cup sugar
1/4 cup baking cocoa
1 teaspoon baking soda
1/2 teaspoon salt
1 cup water
1/3 cup oil
1 tablespoon vinegar
1 teaspoon vanilla extract
8 ounces cream cheese, softened
1 egg
1/3 cup sugar
1/8 teaspoon salt
1 cup chocolate chips
1/4 cup sugar

Sift flour, 1 cup sugar, baking cocoa, baking soda and 1/2 teaspoon salt together in bowl. Add water, oil, vinegar and vanilla; mix well. Pour into 24 paper-lined muffin cups. Combine cream cheese, egg, 1/3 cup sugar and 1/8 teaspoon salt in mixer bowl; beat well. Stir in chocolate chips. Drop by heaping teaspoonfuls onto cupcakes. Bake at 350 degrees for 25 to 30 minutes or until cupcakes test done. Sprinkle with remaining 1/4 cup sugar. Yield: 24 servings.

Approx Per Serving: Cal 181; Prot 2 g; Carbo 24 g; Fiber 1 g;
T Fat 9 g; 45% Calories from Fat; Chol 19 mg; Sod 122 mg.

Lynne Sallinger, Massachusetts

Blueberry Cake

1 1/2 cups flour
1 teaspoon baking powder
1/2 teaspoon salt
1 cup sugar
1/2 cup shortening
2 egg yolks
1/3 cup milk
2 egg whites, stiffly beaten
1 teaspoon vanilla extract
1 1/2 cups floured blueberries
1/4 cup sugar

Sift flour, baking powder and salt together. Cream 1 cup sugar and shortening in mixer bowl until light and fluffy. Beat in egg yolks. Add flour mixture and milk alternately to creamed mixture, beating constantly. Fold in egg whites gently. Stir in vanilla and blueberries. Pour into nonstick 9x13-inch cake pan. Sprinkle with 1/4 cup sugar. Bake at 350 degrees for 35 to 45 minutes or until cake tests done. Yield: 15 servings.

♥ **Approx Per Serving:** Cal 195; Prot 2 g; Carbo 29 g; Fiber 1 g; T Fat 8 g; 36% Calories from Fat; Chol 29 mg; Sod 105 mg.

Jean Fraser, Massachusetts

Carrot Cake

3 cups grated or ground carrots
4 eggs
1 3/4 cups sugar
2 cups flour
1 1/4 cups oil
1 teaspoon salt
2 teaspoons each cinnamon, baking powder and baking soda
1/2 cup chopped pecans
1   10-ounce can crushed pineapple, well drained
4 cups confectioners' sugar
8 ounces cream cheese, softened
1/2 cup butter, softened
2 teaspoons vanilla extract
1/2 cup chopped pecans

Mix carrots, eggs and 1 3/4 cups sugar in bowl. Stir in flour and oil gradually. Add next 4 ingredients; mix well. Stir in 1/2 cup pecans. Pour into 2 greased and floured 9-inch cake pans. Bake at 350 degrees for 30 to 40 minutes or until layers test done. Cool in pans for several minutes. Remove to wire rack to cool completely. Spread 1/3 of the pineapple between layers. Beat next 4 ingredients in mixer bowl until fluffy. Frost cake. Arrange remaining pineapple over frosting. Sprinkle with remaining 1/2 cup pecans. Yield: 16 servings.

♥ **Approx Per Serving:** Cal 613; Prot 5 g; Carbo 74 g; Fiber 2 g; T Fat 35 g; 49% Calories from Fat; Chol 85 mg; Sod 393 mg.

August C. Paoli, Florida

A Vermont Carrot Cake

2 cups flour
2 cups sugar
2 teaspoons baking powder
2 teaspoons baking soda
2 teaspoons cinnamon
1 teaspoon salt
1¼ cups oil
3 cups grated carrots
4 eggs
½ cup chopped pecans
2 teaspoons vanilla extract
4 ounces cream cheese, softened
¼ cup butter, softened
2 cups (or more) confectioners'
 sugar

Combine flour, sugar, baking powder, baking soda, cinnamon and salt in mixer bowl; mix well. Add oil gradually, beating constantly. Stir in carrots. Add eggs 1 at a time, beating well after each addition. Stir in pecans and vanilla. Pour into greased and floured 9x13-inch cake pan. Bake at 350 degrees for 50 to 60 minutes or until cake springs back when lightly touched. Beat cream cheese and butter in mixer bowl until light and fluffy. Beat in enough confectioners' sugar to make of spreading consistency. Spread over cake. Yield: 15 servings.

💜 **Approx Per Serving:** Cal 499; Prot 4 g; Carbo 59 g; Fiber 1 g;
T Fat 28 g; 50% Calories from Fat; Chol 73 mg; Sod 371 mg.

T. Richardson Miner, Jr., Massachusetts

Chocolate-Almond Cake

4 ounces chocolate chips
2 tablespoons brandy
¼ cup canola oil
⅔ cup sugar
5 egg whites
⅓ cup ground almonds
¼ teaspoon vanilla extract
¾ cup sifted flour
2 tablespoons confectioners' sugar

Oil and lightly flour one 8-inch cake pan. Melt chocolate chips in brandy over boiling water in double boiler. Beat oil and sugar in mixer bowl. Beat in egg whites. Stir in almonds, vanilla and flour. Add chocolate mixture; beat well. Pour into prepared pan. Bake at 350 degrees for 25 minutes or until cake tests done. Cool in pan for several minutes. Remove to wire rack to cool completely. Sprinkle with confectioners' sugar. Yield: 8 servings.

💜 **Approx Per Serving:** Cal 325; Prot 6 g; Carbo 39 g; Fiber 2 g;
T Fat 18 g; 47% Calories from Fat; Chol 0 mg; Sod 35 mg.

Gillian Steinhauer, Massachusetts

Chocolate Pudding Cake

2 tablespoons butter
2 ounces unsweetened chocolate
2 cups buttermilk
1 teaspoon vanilla extract
2½ cups unbleached white flour
1 cup packed brown sugar
1 tablespoon baking powder
1 teaspoon baking soda
½ teaspoon salt
1 cup packed brown sugar
10 tablespoons baking cocoa
2½ cups boiling water

Melt butter and chocolate in double boiler. Heat buttermilk in saucepan just until warm; do not boil. Mix chocolate mixture and buttermilk with vanilla in small bowl. Mix next 5 ingredients in large bowl. Stir in chocolate mixture. Spread in greased 9x13-inch cake pan. Sprinkle with mixture of 1 cup brown sugar and baking cocoa. Pour boiling water over top. Bake at 350 degrees for 30 minutes or until center is firm. Let stand for 15 minutes or longer. Serve chocolate side up. Yield: 12 servings.

Approx Per Serving: Cal 326; Prot 5 g; Carbo 67 g; Fiber 2 g; T Fat 6 g; 16% Calories from Fat; Chol 7 mg; Sod 320 mg.

Susan Cammer Gerstein, Massachusetts

Fudge Ribbon Cake

1   2-layer package chocolate cake mix
8 ounces cream cheese, softened
2 tablespoons margarine, softened
1 tablespoon cornstarch
1   14-ounce can sweetened condensed milk
1 egg
1 teaspoon vanilla extract

Prepare cake mix using package directions. Pour into greased and floured 10-inch bundt pan. Beat cream cheese, margarine and cornstarch in mixer bowl until light and fluffy. Add condensed milk, egg and vanilla; mix well. Pour over batter. Bake at 350 degrees for 50 to 55 minutes or until cake tests done. Cool in pan for 10 minutes. Invert onto serving plate. Glaze or garnish as desired. Yield: 16 servings.

Approx Per Serving: Cal 382; Prot 6 g; Carbo 54 g; Fiber <1 g; T Fat 17 g; 38% Calories from Fat; Chol 37 mg; Sod 251 mg.

Lynne Gundersen, Massachusetts

Hungarian Christmas Cake

My family makes this every Christmas.

3¹/₂ cups flour
¹/₈ teaspoon salt
1 teaspoon baking powder
1 cup margarine, softened
1 cup sugar
2 egg yolks
1 teaspoon vanilla extract
1 6-ounce jar raspberry jam
2 egg whites
¹/₂ to 1 cup chopped walnuts

Sift flour, salt and baking powder together. Cream margarine, sugar, egg yolks and vanilla in mixer bowl until light and fluffy. Stir in flour mixture. Press into 10x15-inch cake pan. Spread with jam. Beat egg whites in bowl until foamy. Spread over jam. Sprinkle with walnuts. Bake at 350 degrees for 30 to 45 minutes or until cake tests done. Cool. Cut into 3-inch squares. Yield: 20 servings.

♥ **Approx Per Serving:** Cal 270; Prot 4 g; Carbo 34 g; Fiber 1 g; T Fat 14 g; 45% Calories from Fat; Chol 21 mg; Sod 145 mg.

Margaret Stetler, Massachusetts

Irish Cakes

This recipe came from my mother, who is Irish.

4 cups flour
2 teaspoons baking soda
1 pound raisins
1¹/₂ cups sugar
1 cup margarine
2¹/₂ cups cold water
¹/₈ teaspoon salt
1 teaspoon nutmeg
1 teaspoon mace
1 teaspoon allspice
1 teaspoon cinnamon
2 to 4 eggs, beaten

Sift flour and baking soda together. Combine raisins, sugar, margarine, water, salt and spices in saucepan. Bring to a boil. Simmer for 10 minutes. Let stand until cool. Stir eggs into flour mixture. Add raisin mixture; mix well. Pour into 2 greased and floured loaf pans or 1 tube pan. Bake at 350 degrees for 1 hour or until cake tests done. Yield: 16 servings.

♥ **Approx Per Serving:** Cal 383; Prot 5 g; Carbo 65 g; Fiber 3 g; T Fat 13 g; 29% Calories from Fat; Chol 27 mg; Sod 266 mg.

Mrs. William G. Richeimer, Sr., Connecticut

Chocolate-Buttermilk Pound Cake

³/4 cup butter, softened
1¹/2 cups sugar
2 eggs
1 teaspoon vanilla extract
³/4 cup sour cream
2 cups flour
²/3 cup baking cocoa
2 teaspoons baking soda
1 cup buttermilk

Cream butter, sugar, eggs and vanilla in mixer bowl until light and fluffy. Stir in sour cream. Add mixture of flour and baking cocoa. Dissolve baking soda in buttermilk. Stir into batter. Beat for 2 minutes. Pour into greased and floured bundt pan. Bake at 350 degrees for 40 to 45 minutes or until cake tests done. Cool in pan for several minutes. Invert onto serving plate. Yield: 16 servings.

♥ **Approx Per Serving:** Cal 255; Prot 4 g; Carbo 34 g; Fiber 1 g; T Fat 13 g; 43% Calories from Fat; Chol 55 mg; Sod 207 mg.

Pam Hurlbert, New Hampshire

Hummingbird Cake

This recipe is a family favorite.

3 cups flour
1 teaspoon baking soda
1 teaspoon salt
1 teaspoon cinnamon
2 cups sugar
1 cup oil
3 eggs, lightly beaten
1   8-ounce can crushed pineapple
2 cups mashed bananas
1   3-ounce can flaked coconut
1¹/2 teaspoons vanilla extract

Sift flour, baking soda, salt, cinnamon and sugar together. Combine oil, eggs, undrained pineapple and bananas in bowl; mix well. Add flour mixture; stir just until mixed. Stir in coconut and vanilla. Pour into buttered and floured 10-inch tube pan with removable bottom. Bake at 350 degrees for 1 hour and 10 minutes. Cool cake in pan on wire rack for 15 minutes. Remove side of pan. Cool completely. Invert onto serving plate. Yield: 16 servings.

♥ **Approx Per Serving:** Cal 379; Prot 4 g; Carbo 55 g; Fiber 2 g; T Fat 17 g; 39% Calories from Fat; Chol 40 mg; Sod 200 mg.

Peggy Kelley, Massachusetts

Nana's Famous Cake

3 cups flour
1 tablespoon baking powder
1 cup butter, softened
2 cups sugar
4 egg yolks
2 teaspoons vanilla extract
1 cup milk
4 egg whites
1/8 teaspoon cream of tartar

Sift flour and baking powder together. Cream butter and sugar in mixer bowl for 10 to 15 minutes or until light and fluffy. Beat in egg yolks. Stir in vanilla. Add flour mixture and milk alternately to creamed mixture, beating well after each addition. Beat egg whites with cream of tartar in mixer bowl until stiff but not dry. Fold gently into batter. Pour into greased and floured angel food cake pan. Bake at 350 degrees for 1 hour. Yield: 16 servings.

♥ **Approx Per Serving:** Cal 315; Prot 5 g; Carbo 44 g; Fiber 1 g; T Fat 14 g; 39% Calories from Fat; Chol 86 mg; Sod 180 mg.

Elaine M. Pfeifer, Massachusetts

Passover Sponge Cake

8 eggs, separated
11/2 cups sugar
Juice of 1 lemon
3/4 teaspoon salt
3/4 cup potato starch
1/4 cup cake meal

Beat egg whites with 1/2 cup sugar in mixer bowl until stiff. Beat egg yolks for 5 minutes in mixer bowl. Add 1 cup sugar, beating constantly until sugar is dissolved. Stir in lemon juice and salt. Fold in egg whites. Stir in potato starch and cake meal. Pour into tube pan. Bake at 325 degrees for 1 hour. Invert cake in pan onto bottle for 1 hour or until cool. Invert cake onto cake plate. Yield: 16 servings.

♥ **Approx Per Serving:** Cal 144; Prot 3 g; Carbo 27 g; Fiber <1 g; T Fat 3 g; 17% Calories from Fat; Chol 106 mg; Sod 138 mg.

Elaine Weiner, Massachusetts

Oatmeal-Caramel Loaf Cake

This is an old family recipe handed down from Wales. It is a moist, delicious cake that is great for family get-togethers. The frosting tastes like penuche.

1 cup oats
1½ cups boiling water
1 cup sugar
1 cup packed light brown sugar
½ cup margarine, softened
2 eggs
1 teaspoon salt
1 teaspoon baking soda
1 teaspoon baking powder
1½ cups flour
1 teaspoon vanilla extract
1 teaspoon cinnamon
½ cup margarine
½ cup evaporated milk
1 cup packed light brown sugar
1 teaspoon vanilla extract
⅔ to 1 cup sifted confectioners' sugar
1 cup shredded coconut

Combine oats and boiling water in bowl. Let stand for 30 minutes. Add sugar, 1 cup brown sugar, ½ cup margarine, eggs, salt, baking soda, baking powder, flour, 1 teaspoon vanilla and cinnamon; mix well. Pour into 8x10-inch cake pan. Bake at 325 degrees for 45 minutes. Combine ½ cup margarine, evaporated milk, 1 cup brown sugar and 1 teaspoon vanilla in saucepan. Bring to a soft boil; remove from heat. Add enough confectioners' sugar to make of spreading consistency. Fold in coconut. Spread over cooled cake. Yield: 36 servings.

Approx Per Serving: Cal 186; Prot 1 g; Carbo 31 g; Fiber 1 g; T Fat 7 g; 34% Calories from Fat; Chol 13 mg; Sod 172 mg.

Mrs. Myron Purdy, New York

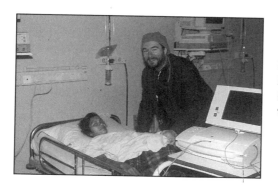

Dr. David Martin, co-chair of Lahey Clinic's Global Outreach Committee and a Project Pacer volunteer with a patient in India

Shaker Pineapple Cake

This recipe was taken from my great-grandmother Achsah Ward's "Kitchen Logg" dated 1823. It was updated using modern measurements.

2 eggs
1 20-ounce can crushed pineapple
2¼ cups flour, sifted
2 cups sugar
2 teaspoons baking soda
1 cup chopped walnuts
2 cups confectioners' sugar, sifted 3 times
4 ounces cream cheese, softened
2 tablespoons whipping cream
2 teaspoons vanilla extract
¾ cup chopped walnuts

Beat eggs in bowl. Add undrained pineapple, flour, sugar and baking soda; beat well. Stir in 1 cup walnuts. Pour into ungreased 9x13-inch cake pan. Draw batter away from edges and toward center of pan with spatula. Bake at 350 degrees for 40 minutes or until cake tests done. Cool. Beat next 4 ingredients in mixer bowl until smooth. Stir in ¾ cup walnuts. Frost cake. Yield: 15 servings.

♥ **Approx Per Serving:** Cal 397; Prot 6 g; Carbo 67 g; Fiber 2 g; T Fat 13 g; 29% Calories from Fat; Chol 39 mg; Sod 145 mg.

Russell Ward Nadeau, Massachusetts

Lemon-Poppy Seed Cake

2½ cups flour
½ teaspoon baking powder
1 teaspoon baking soda
1 cup sugar
1 cup low-fat margarine, softened
Egg substitute equivalent to 3 eggs
1½ teaspoons lemon extract
1 cup low-fat lemon yogurt
⅓ cup poppy seed

Sift flour, baking powder and baking soda together. Cream sugar and margarine in mixer bowl until light and fluffy. Beat in egg substitute. Stir in flavoring. Beat in flour mixture and yogurt alternately. Stir in poppy seed. Pour into greased and floured bundt pan. Bake at 350 degrees for 45 to 50 minutes or until cake tests done. Cool in pan for 10 minutes. Invert onto cake plate. Yield: 16 servings.

♥ **Approx Per Serving:** Cal 206; Prot 5 g; Carbo 30 g; Fiber 1 g; T Fat 8 g; 33% Calories from Fat; Chol 1 mg; Sod 227 mg.

Rebecca F. McMenimen, Massachusetts

Pumpkin Roll Cake

3/4 cup flour
1 teaspoon baking powder
2 teaspoons cinnamon
1 teaspoon ginger
1/2 teaspoon nutmeg
1/2 teaspoon salt
3 eggs
1 cup sugar
2/3 cup canned pumpkin
1 teaspoon lemon juice
1 cup finely chopped walnuts
1 cup confectioners' sugar
6 ounces cream cheese, softened
1/4 cup butter, softened
1/2 teaspoon vanilla extract

Grease 10x15-inch cake roll pan. Line with greased waxed paper. Sift first 6 ingredients together. Beat eggs at high speed in mixer bowl for 5 minutes. Add sugar gradually, beating constantly. Stir in pumpkin and lemon juice. Spread evenly in prepared pan. Sprinkle with walnuts. Bake at 375 degrees for 12 to 15 minutes or until cake tests done. Invert onto towel sprinkled with confectioners' sugar. Remove waxed paper. Roll up cake and towel as for jelly roll. Cool completely. Unroll; remove towel. Beat 1 cup confectioners' sugar, cream cheese, butter and vanilla in mixer bowl until smooth. Spread over cooled cake. Reroll cake. Place on serving plate. Yield: 20 servings.

Approx Per Serving: Cal 182; Prot 3 g; Carbo 22 g; Fiber 1 g; T Fat 10 g; 47% Calories from Fat; Chol 47 mg; Sod 126 mg.

G. Frances Hansen, Massachusetts

Group of volunteers on a Christian Medical and Dental Society mission in Mexico

Swedish Nut Cake

This has been a Christmas favorite of our family for many years.

3 cups flour
2 teaspoons baking powder
2 cups sugar
1 cup butter, softened
4 egg yolks, beaten
1 cup milk
1 teaspoon vanilla extract
1 cup walnuts
1/4 cup flour
4 egg whites, stiffly beaten

Sift flour and baking powder together. Cream sugar and butter in mixer bowl until light and fluffy. Add egg yolks; beat well. Add flour mixture and milk alternately to creamed mixture, beating well after each addition. Stir in vanilla. Add mixture of walnuts and 1/4 cup flour; mix well. Fold in egg whites. Pour into greased and floured 9x13-inch cake pan. Bake at 350 degrees for 35 to 40 minutes or until cake tests done. Spread with favorite vanilla frosting. Garnish with chopped walnuts. Yield: 15 servings.

♥ **Approx Per Serving:** Cal 394; Prot 6 g; Carbo 50 g; Fiber 1 g; T Fat 20 g; 44% Calories from Fat; Chol 92 mg; Sod 171 mg.

Carolyn Gould, Massachusetts

Tomato Soup Cake

1 10-ounce can tomato soup
1 teaspoon baking soda
2 cups flour
2 teaspoons baking powder
1/4 teaspoon salt
1 teaspoon cinnamon
1/2 teaspoon nutmeg
1/4 teaspoon cloves
1 cup sugar
1/2 cup shortening

Mix tomato soup and baking soda in bowl; set aside. Sift next 6 ingredients together. Cream sugar and shortening in mixer bowl until light and fluffy. Add soup mixture and flour mixture alternately, beating well after each addition. Pour into greased and floured 8x8-inch cake pan. Bake at 350 degrees for 25 to 30 minutes or until cake tests done. Spread with favorite cream cheese frosting. Yield: 8 servings.

♥ **Approx Per Serving:** Cal 349; Prot 4 g; Carbo 54 g; Fiber 1 g; T Fat 14 g; 35% Calories from Fat; Chol 0 mg; Sod 499 mg.

Winona D. Jones, Maine

Almond Biscotti

*John Libertino is fond of biscotti dipped in coffee with lots of milk.
He tries to have only one at a time—but that idea never works.*

1/2 cup butter, softened
1 cup sugar
2 eggs
1/2 teaspoon vanilla extract
1/4 teaspoon almond extract
1 teaspoon grated orange rind
2 1/2 cups flour
1 1/2 teaspoons baking powder
1/2 teaspoon salt
1 teaspoon cloves
1 teaspoon mace
1 1/2 cups coarsely chopped almonds
1/2 cup golden raisins
1 egg
1 tablespoon water

Cream butter and sugar in mixer bowl until light and fluffy. Beat in 2 eggs 1 at a time. Add flavorings; mix well. Add mixture of next 5 ingredients; beat well. Stir in almonds and raisins. Shape into two 1 1/2x14-inch rolls. Place 3 inches apart on cookie sheet. Beat remaining egg with 1 tablespoon water. Brush over rolls. Bake at 325 degrees for 45 minutes or until golden brown. Cool slightly. Cut into 1/2-inch slices. Place cut side up on cookie sheet. Bake at 250 degrees for 40 minutes or until dry. Yield: 56 servings.

♥ **Approx Per Serving:** Cal 78; Prot 2 g; Carbo 10 g; Fiber 1 g;
T Fat 4 g; 46% Calories from Fat; Chol 16 mg; Sod 46 mg.

Mary Jo Libertino, Massachusetts

Bergin's Best Brownies

1 cup sugar
3/4 cup flour
1/2 cup vegetable oil
1 teaspoon vanilla extract
1/2 teaspoon salt
1/2 teaspoon baking powder
2 eggs, beaten
2　1-ounce packages Nestle's unsweetened chocolate
1 cup chopped walnuts
1/2 cup shredded coconut

Combine sugar, flour, oil, vanilla, salt and baking powder in bowl; mix well. Beat in eggs. Heat chocolate under running water. Add chocolate to mixture; mix well. Stir in walnuts and coconut. Spread in greased 9x9-inch baking dish. Bake at 350 degrees for 20 to 25 minutes or until edges pull from side of dish.
Yield: 9 servings.

♥ **Approx Per Serving:** Cal 394; Prot 5 g; Carbo 37 g; Fiber 3 g;
T Fat 27 g; 59% Calories from Fat; Chol 47 mg; Sod 168 mg.

Terry Hale, Massachusetts

Unbaked Buckeyes

2 cups butter, softened
2　16-ounce jars creamy peanut
　　butter
3 pounds confectioners' sugar
2 cups semisweet chocolate chips

Combine butter and peanut butter in bowl; mix well. Add confectioners' sugar gradually, beating well. Shape into 1-inch balls; place on waxed paper. Chill for 1 hour. Melt chocolate chips in double boiler over hot water, stirring until smooth. Dip half of each ball into chocolate; place on waxed paper. Chill for 30 to 60 minutes. Yield: 140 servings.

💜 **Approx Per Serving:** Cal 119; Prot 2 g; Carbo 14 g; Fiber <1 g;
　　T Fat 7 g; 49% Calories from Fat; Chol 7 mg; Sod 49 mg.

Lee M. Cappucci, Massachusetts

Chocolate-Peanut Butter Cookies

1 1/2 cups packed brown sugar
1 cup peanut butter
3/4 cup margarine, softened
1/3 cup water
1 egg
1 teaspoon vanilla extract
3 cups oats
1 1/2 cups flour
1/2 teaspoon baking soda
1 1/2 cups semisweet chocolate chips
4 teaspoons vegetable shortening
1/3 cup chopped pecans

Cream first 3 ingredients in bowl until light and fluffy. Add water, egg and vanilla; mix well. Add mixture of oats, flour and baking soda; mix well. Shape into 1-inch balls. Place on ungreased cookie sheet. Flatten to 1/4-inch thickness with bottom of glass dipped in sugar. Bake at 350 degrees for 8 to 10 minutes or until cookies test done. Cool on cookie sheet for several minutes. Remove to wire rack to cool completely. Heat chocolate chips and shortening in saucepan over low heat until chocolate is melted, stirring frequently. Top each cookie with 1/2 teaspoon chocolate; sprinkle with pecans. Chill until set. Yield: 72 servings.

💜 **Approx Per Serving:** Cal 107; Prot 2 g; Carbo 13 g; Fiber 1 g;
　　T Fat 6 g; 48% Calories from Fat; Chol 3 mg; Sod 47 mg.

Mary Ellen Iorio, Massachusetts

Chocolate-Raspberry-Hazelnut Macaroon Bars

1 ounce unsweetened chocolate,
  melted
1/2 cup sugar
1/4 cup melted unsalted butter
1 egg
1/2 teaspoon vanilla extract
1/3 cup flour
Salt to taste
1/2 cup seedless raspberry jam
2 tablespoons orange liqueur
2 cups blanched hazelnuts, toasted
11/2 cups sugar
1/2 teaspoon salt
6 egg whites
1 teaspoon vanilla extract

Combine chocolate, 1/2 cup sugar, butter and egg in bowl; mix well. Add next 3 ingredients; mix well. Grease 9x13-inch baking dish; sprinkle with baking cocoa. Spread mixture in baking dish. Bake at 350 degrees for 10 minutes. Cool in pan for 5 minutes. Spread mixture of jam and liqueur over baked layer, leaving 1/2-inch border around edge. Grind hazelnuts with 11/2 cups sugar and 1/2 teaspoon salt in food processor until very fine. Add egg whites and 1 teaspoon vanilla. Process until well combined. Spoon over top, spreading to edge. Bake at 375 degrees for 25 to 30 minutes or until light brown. Cool. Cut into bars. Yield: 36 servings.

♥ **Approx Per Serving:** Cal 131; Prot 2 g; Carbo 17 g; Fiber 1 g; T Fat 7 g; 44% Calories from Fat; Chol 9 mg; Sod 41 mg.

Sylvia Tolman, Massachusetts

Dinosaur Chow

1/4 cup dirt (baking cocoa)
1/2 cup swamp water (milk with
  green food coloring)
2 cups crushed bones (sugar)
1/2 cup fat (melted butter)
2 cups dead grass (oats)
1/2 cup squashed bugs (peanut
  butter)

Bring first 4 ingredients to a boil in saucepan; reduce heat. Simmer for 3 minutes, stirring frequently. Add grass and bugs; mix well. Remove from heat. Stir until mixture thickens. Drop by teaspoonfuls onto waxed-paper lined tray. Cool. Yield: 60 servings.

♥ **Approx Per Serving:** Cal 65; Prot 1 g; Carbo 9 g; Fiber 1 g; T Fat 3 g; 39% Calories from Fat; Chol 4 mg; Sod 23 mg.

Elaine Bergeron, Massachusetts

Fruit Bars

1 cup sugar
3 eggs
1 1/2 teaspoons vanilla extract
1/2 cup corn oil
3 cups flour
1 1/2 teaspoons baking powder
1 cup chocolate chips
1/2 cup chopped walnuts
20 maraschino cherries, chopped
2 teaspoons maraschino cherry juice

Combine sugar, eggs, vanilla and oil in bowl; mix well. Mix flour and baking powder together. Add to mixture; mix well. Stir in chocolate chips, walnuts, maraschino cherries and juice. Spread in 3 rectangles on greased cookie sheet. Bake at 350 degrees for 20 to 25 minutes or until golden brown. Cut into bars while still warm. Yield: 20 servings.

♥ **Approx Per Serving:** Cal 237; Prot 4 g; Carbo 32 g; Fiber 1 g;
T Fat 11 g; 42% Calories from Fat; Chol 32 mg; Sod 37 mg.

Francine DeFrancesco, Massachusetts

English Holiday Cookies

2 egg whites
8 ounces ground almonds
1/2 cup superfine sugar
1 tablespoon cinnamon
1 cup sifted confectioners' sugar

Beat egg whites in mixer bowl until stiff peaks form. Fold in almonds, sugar and cinnamon. Shape into 1-inch balls with wet hands. Place on greased cookie sheet. Bake at 325 degrees for 25 minutes or until just firm to touch. Do not overbake. Best when soft inside. Roll in confectioners' sugar while still warm. Cool on wire rack. Roll in confectioners' sugar again. Yield: 24 servings.

♥ **Approx Per Serving:** Cal 90; Prot 2 g; Carbo 10 g; Fiber 1 g;
T Fat 5 g; 47% Calories from Fat; Chol 0 mg; Sod 5 mg.

David T. Martin, M.D., Massachusetts

Chewy Gingersnaps

³/4 cup margarine
1 cup sugar
1 egg
¹/4 cup molasses
¹/8 teaspoon salt
2 cups flour
2 teaspoons baking soda
¹/2 teaspoon cloves
1 teaspoon cinnamon
1 teaspoon ginger
1 cup sugar

Cream margarine and 1 cup sugar in mixer bowl until light and fluffy. Add egg; beat well. Add molasses; mix well. Sift salt, flour, baking soda and spices together. Add to creamed mixture; mix well. Shape into 1-inch balls with wet hands; roll in 1 cup sugar. Place on nonstick cookie sheet. Bake at 350 degrees for 10 to 12 minutes or until brown around edge but still soft in center. Do not overbake. Cool on cookie sheet for several minutes. Remove to wire rack to cool completely. Yield: 24 servings.

♥ **Approx Per Serving:** Cal 164; Prot 1 g; Carbo 27 g; Fiber <1 g; T Fat 6 g; 33% Calories from Fat; Chol 9 mg; Sod 151 mg.

Harriet Bennett, Massachusetts

Thin Molasses Cookies

¹/2 cup margarine, softened
¹/2 cup shortening
1 cup sugar
1 egg
¹/4 cup molasses
2 cups flour
2 teaspoons baking soda
¹/2 teaspoon salt
1 teaspoon cinnamon
1 teaspoon cloves
1¹/2 teaspoons ginger

Cream margarine, shortening and sugar in mixer bowl until light and fluffy. Add egg and molasses; beat well. Mix flour and remaining ingredients together. Add to creamed mixture; mix well. Drop by teaspoonfuls onto nonstick cookie sheet. Bake at 350 degrees for 7 minutes or until cookies test done. Cool on cookie sheet for several minutes. Remove to wire rack to cool completely. Yield: 24 servings.

♥ **Approx Per Serving:** Cal 152; Prot 1 g; Carbo 18 g; Fiber <1 g; T Fat 8 g; 49% Calories from Fat; Chol 9 mg; Sod 161 mg.

Mrs. John L. McCrea, Massachusetts

Frosted Pumpkin-Spice Cookies

1/2 cup shortening
1 cup sugar
2 eggs, beaten
1 cup solid-pack pumpkin
2 cups sifted flour
1 teaspoon baking powder
1 teaspoon salt
2 1/2 teaspoons cinnamon
1/2 teaspoon nutmeg
1/4 teaspoon ginger
1 cup raisins
1 cup chopped pecans
2 cups confectioners' sugar
1 tablespoon lemon juice
1 tablespoon grated lemon rind
1/4 cup (about) milk

Cream shortening and sugar in mixer bowl until light and fluffy. Add eggs and pumpkin; mix well. Sift flour, baking powder, salt and spices together. Add to pumpkin mixture. Stir in raisins and pecans. Drop by heaping teaspoonfuls onto greased cookie sheet. Bake at 350 degrees for 15 minutes or until cookies are firm to touch. Cool on cookie sheet for several minutes. Remove to wire rack to cool completely. Combine confectioners' sugar, lemon juice and rind in mixer bowl. Beat in just enough milk to make of spreading consistency. Spread on cookies. Yield: 48 servings.

♥ **Approx Per Serving:** Cal 105; Prot 1 g; Carbo 17 g; Fiber 1 g;
T Fat 4 g; 35% Calories from Fat; Chol 9 mg; Sod 56 mg.

Judy Trant, Massachusetts

Snickerdoodles

*These have been a favorite of my children for over 20 years. I can't
wait to make them for my new grandson, Nathan.*

1 cup margarine, softened
1 1/2 cups sugar
2 eggs
2 1/2 cups flour
1 teaspoon cinnamon
1 teaspoon baking soda
1/4 teaspoon salt
2 teaspoons cream of tartar
1/4 cup cinnamon-sugar

Cream margarine and sugar in mixer bowl until light and fluffy. Beat in eggs. Add mixture of next 5 ingredients; mix well. Chill for 1 hour. Shape by teaspoonfuls into balls. Roll in cinnamon-sugar. Place on foil-lined cookie sheet. Bake at 325 degrees for 10 minutes or until light brown on bottom. Cool on wire rack. Yield: 48 servings.

♥ **Approx Per Serving:** Cal 89; Prot 1 g; Carbo 12 g; Fiber <1 g;
T Fat 4 g; 41% Calories from Fat; Chol 9 mg; Sod 76 mg.

Patty Sumner, Massachusetts

Tasty Texas Squares

1 cup water
¹/4 cup (rounded) baking cocoa
1 cup butter
2 cups each sugar and flour
¹/2 teaspoon salt
1 teaspoon baking soda
2 eggs, beaten
¹/2 cup sour cream
¹/4 cup (rounded) baking cocoa
6 tablespoons milk
¹/2 cup butter
1 teaspoon vanilla extract
4 cups (about) confectioners' sugar
24 Hershey's Kisses candies

Bring first 3 ingredients to a boil in saucepan, stirring frequently. Remove from heat. Add sugar, flour, salt, baking soda, eggs and sour cream; mix well. Pour into greased 10x15-inch baking pan. Bake at 400 degrees for 12 to 15 minutes. Cool. Bring ¹/4 cup cocoa, milk and ¹/2 cup butter to a boil in saucepan, stirring frequently. Remove from heat. Add vanilla and enough confectioners' sugar to make of spreading consistency. Frost baked layer. Cut into 2-inch squares. Top each with candy. Yield: 24 servings.

♥ **Approx Per Serving:** Cal 341; Prot 3 g; Carbo 51 g; Fiber 2 g;
   T Fat 15 g; 39% Calories from Fat; Chol 52 mg; Sod 191 mg.

Kerry J. Hughes, Massachusetts

Whoopee Pie Cookies

1 cup butter, softened
2 cups sugar
2 eggs
2 teaspoons vanilla extract
4 cups flour
1 cup baking cocoa
1 tablespoon baking soda
1 teaspoon baking powder
1 teaspoon salt
2 cups milk
1¹/2 cups melted butter
1¹/2 teaspoons vanilla extract
1¹/2 13-ounce jars marshmallow
   creme
4 cups confectioners' sugar

Cream 1 cup butter and sugar in mixer bowl until light and fluffy. Add eggs and 2 teaspoons vanilla; mix well. Mix flour, cocoa, baking soda, baking powder and salt together. Add milk and flour mixture to creamed mixture; mix well. Drop by teaspoonfuls onto greased cookie sheet. Bake at 400 degrees for 7 to 8 minutes or until edges are brown. Cool. Beat 1¹/2 cups butter and remaining ingredients in mixer bowl until smooth. Frost cookies.
Yield: 40 servings.

♥ **Approx Per Serving:** Cal 300; Prot 3 g; Carbo 46 g; Fiber 1 g;
   T Fat 13 g; 37% Calories from Fat; Chol 43 mg; Sod 237 mg.

Shawn P. Middleton, Massachusetts

Dutch Apple Pie

1/4 cup whipping cream
1/2 teaspoon white vinegar
1 recipe 1-crust pie pastry
3 cups apple wedges
1/4 cup flour
1 teaspoon cinnamon
1 cup packed brown sugar
1/4 cup butter

Combine cream and vinegar in bowl; mix well. Let stand at room temperature for 30 minutes. Line 9-inch pie plate with pie pastry. Arrange apple wedges in prepared pie plate. Combine flour, cinnamon and brown sugar in bowl; mix well. Cut in butter until crumbly. Sprinkle over apples. Pour in cream mixture. Bake at 425 degrees for 10 minutes. Reduce oven temperature to 350 degrees. Bake for 40 minutes longer or until apples are tender. Serve warm with whipped cream.
Yield: 8 servings.

Approx Per Serving: Cal 356; Prot 2 g; Carbo 52 g; Fiber 1 g; T Fat 16 g; 40% Calories from Fat; Chol 26 mg; Sod 204 mg.

Mrs. G. W. F. McCain, Canada

Swedish Apple Pie

6 medium apples
1 tablespoon sugar
1 tablespoon cinnamon
1 cup sugar
1 cup flour
1 egg
10 tablespoons plus 2 teaspoons
   melted margarine

Peel, core and slice apples. Combine 1 tablespoon sugar and cinnamon in bowl; mix well. Add apples, tossing to coat with mixture. Pour into 9-inch pie plate. Combine sugar and flour in bowl; mix well. Add egg and margarine; mix well. Pour over apples. Bake at 350 degrees for 1 hour or until top is brown and apples are tender. Yield: 8 servings.

Approx Per Serving: Cal 719; Prot 5 g; Carbo 99 g; Fiber 4 g; T Fat 35 g; 43% Calories from Fat; Chol 1 mg; Sod 369 mg.

Karen Sanderson, Massachusetts

Chupal's Succulent Apple Pie

1/2 cup packed light brown sugar
2/3 cup sugar
1/4 cup flour
2 teaspoons cinnamon
3/4 teaspoon nutmeg
3/4 teaspoon ginger
6 large McIntosh apples, peeled, sliced
2 cups flour
1 teaspoon salt
1 cup shortening
1/4 cup cold water
2 tablespoons butter
2 tablespoons milk

Mix first 6 ingredients in bowl. Add apples, tossing to coat. Mix 2 cups flour and salt in bowl. Cut in shortening until crumbly. Add cold water, tossing to mix. Divide into 2 portions. Roll each portion into 12-inch circle on lightly floured surface. Fit half the pastry into 9-inch pie plate. Moisten edge with water. Add apple mixture to pie pastry. Dot with butter. Top with remaining pastry, sealing edge and cutting vent. Brush top with milk. Bake at 450 degrees for 10 minutes. Reduce oven temperature to 400 degrees. Bake for 30 minutes longer. Yield: 8 servings.

♥ **Approx Per Serving:** Cal 539; Prot 4 g; Carbo 74 g; Fiber 3 g; T Fat 26 g; 43% Calories from Fat; Chol 1 mg; Sod 277 mg.

Charlotte Melillo, New Hampshire

Cheesecake Pie

16 ounces cream cheese, softened
1/2 cup sugar
1/2 teaspoon vanilla extract
4 eggs
2 cups sour cream
1/3 cup sugar
1/4 teaspoon vanilla extract

Combine cream cheese and 1/2 cup sugar in bowl; mix well. Add 1/2 teaspoon vanilla. Beat in eggs 1 at a time. Pour into buttered 10-inch pie plate. Bake at 325 degrees for 35 minutes. Cool for 25 minutes. Beat remaining ingredients in bowl. Pour over pie. Bake for 20 minutes longer. Chill until serving time. Yield: 8 servings.

♥ **Approx Per Serving:** Cal 442; Prot 9 g; Carbo 25 g; Fiber 0 g; T Fat 35 g; 70% Calories from Fat; Chol 194 mg; Sod 233 mg.

David J. Bryan, M.D., Massachusetts

Ricotta Pie

64 ounces ricotta cheese
4 eggs
2 teaspoons vanilla extract
1   1-pound package confectioners'
    sugar
4 cups sifted flour
Salt to taste
1 tablespoon baking powder
1 cup sugar
1/2 cup shortening
2 eggs
1 egg white
1 teaspoon vanilla extract
1 egg yolk
1 tablespoon milk

Combine ricotta cheese, 4 eggs and 2 teaspoons vanilla in mixer bowl; beat well. Add confectioners' sugar, beating until smooth and creamy. Combine flour, salt, baking powder and sugar in bowl; mix well. Cut in shortening until crumbly. Add 2 eggs, 1 egg white and 1 teaspoon vanilla; mix well. Divide into 4 portions. Roll out each portion on floured surface into 12-inch circle. Fit pastry into two 9-inch pie plates. Add ricotta cheese mixture. Top with remaining pastry, sealing edge and cutting vents. Combine remaining egg yolk with milk in bowl; brush onto top of pies. Bake at 325 degrees for 1 to 1 1/2 hours or until brown. May cut top pastry into strips and arrange lattice-fashion on top. Yield: 16 servings.

♥ **Approx Per Serving:** Cal 577; Prot 19 g; Carbo 72 g; Fiber 1 g; T Fat 24 g; 37% Calories from Fat; Chol 151 mg; Sod 188 mg.

Angel Bova, Massachusetts

*Young patient
in El Salvador with
occular foreign/body
corneal ulcer*

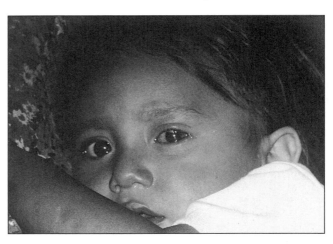

Chocolate-Almond-Ricotta Pie

1¼ cups graham cracker crumbs
2 tablespoons sugar
4 to 6 tablespoons melted margarine
16 ounces ricotta cheese
¾ cup sugar
1 teaspoon almond extract
1 cup toasted almonds, chilled
½ cup semisweet chocolate chips, chilled
1½ cups whipping cream, whipped

Combine graham cracker crumbs and 2 tablespoons sugar in bowl; mix well. Add enough margarine to mix well. Press onto bottom and up sides of 9-inch pie plate. Chill in refrigerator. Combine ricotta cheese, ¾ cup sugar and almond extract in bowl; mix well. Combine almonds and chocolate chips ⅓ at a time in blender container, processing until medium fine. Chill in refrigerator until mixing time to avoid chocolate melting. Fold into ricotta cheese mixture. Fold in whipped cream ½ at a time. Spoon into chilled crust, smoothing top. Chill for several hours to overnight before serving. Yield: 8 servings.

♥ **Approx Per Serving:** Cal 645; Prot 13 g; Carbo 49 g; Fiber 3 g; T Fat 47 g; 63% Calories from Fat; Chol 90 mg; Sod 284 mg.

Muriel J. MacKenzie, Connecticut

Cranberry and Coconut Pie

2 cups cranberries
⅓ cup sugar
⅓ cup coconut
1 egg, beaten
½ cup sugar
½ cup flour
4 to 6 tablespoons melted butter

Spread cranberries in buttered 8-inch pie plate. Sprinkle with ⅓ cup sugar and coconut. Combine egg, ½ cup sugar, flour and melted butter in bowl; mix well. Pour over cranberries. Bake at 350 degrees for 40 to 55 minutes or until golden brown. Serve warm with ice cream or yogurt. Yield: 6 servings.

♥ **Approx Per Serving:** Cal 294; Prot 2 g; Carbo 41 g; Fiber 2 g; T Fat 14 g; 42% Calories from Fat; Chol 67 mg; Sod 110 mg.

Barbara Krey, New Hampshire

Crunchy Ice Cream Pie

1/2 cup melted butter
1 cup packed brown sugar
3 cups cornflakes
1 cup chopped pecans
1 cup shredded coconut
1 quart vanilla ice cream, slightly
  softened

Combine butter and brown sugar in bowl; mix well. Stir in cornflakes, pecans and coconut. Press 2/3 of mixture onto bottom and up sides of 9-inch pie plate. Spoon ice cream into prepared pie plate. Sprinkle remaining 1/3 mixture over top. Freeze overnight. Serve with hot fudge sauce. Yield: 8 servings.

♥ **Approx Per Serving:** Cal 555; Prot 5 g; Carbo 65 g; Fiber 2 g;
  T Fat 33 g; 52% Calories from Fat; Chol 61 mg; Sod 306 mg.

Eva L. Carlson, Massachusetts

Jackie's Bluegrass Chocolate Chip Pie

*Jackie, a very dear friend, grew up in Kentucky and attended
the Kentucky Derby each year.*

2 eggs
1/2 teaspoon salt
1/2 cup butter, softened
1 cup flour
1 cup sugar
2 to 3 tablespoons bourbon
1 cup walnuts
1 cup chocolate chips
1 unbaked 9-inch pie shell

Combine eggs, salt and butter in mixer bowl; beat well. Add flour, sugar and bourbon; mix well. Stir in walnuts and chocolate chips. Spoon into pie shell. Bake at 350 degrees for 30 minutes. May substitute vanilla extract for bourbon and pecans for walnuts. Yield: 8 servings.

♥ **Approx Per Serving:** Cal 618; Prot 8 g; Carbo 63 g; Fiber 2 g;
  T Fat 38 g; 54% Calories from Fat; Chol 84 mg; Sod 390 mg.

Marlene E. Johansen, Massachusetts

Heavenly Pie

4 egg whites
1/4 teaspoon cream of tartar
1 cup sugar
1/4 teaspoon salt
1 teaspoon vanilla extract
4 egg yolks
1/2 cup sugar
1/4 cup lemon juice
1/8 teaspoon salt
1 1/4 cups whipping cream, whipped

Beat egg whites in mixer bowl until soft peaks form. Add cream of tartar, 1 cup sugar, 1/4 teaspoon salt and vanilla gradually, beating until stiff. Spoon into greased 9-inch pie plate. Bake at 275 degrees for 30 minutes. Increase oven temperature to 300 degrees. Bake for 30 minutes longer. Beat egg yolks in mixer bowl. Add sugar gradually, mixing well. Add lemon juice and 1/8 teaspoon salt. Pour into double boiler. Cook over boiling water for 5 to 8 minutes or until thickened, stirring constantly. Cool. Fold in 1 cup whipped cream. Pour into pie crust. Top with remaining whipped cream. Chill until serving time. Yield: 8 servings.

♥ **Approx Per Serving:** Cal 316; Prot 4 g; Carbo 39 g; Fiber <1 g; T Fat 17 g; 46% Calories from Fat; Chol 157 mg; Sod 144 mg.

Martha S. Fleming, Massachusetts

Old South Lemon Meringue Pie

1/2 cup lemon juice
1 teaspoon grated lemon rind
1   14-ounce can sweetened
    condensed milk
3 egg yolks
1 baked 8-inch pie shell, chilled
3 egg whites
1/4 teaspoon cream of tartar
1/4 cup sugar

Combine lemon juice and rind in mixer bowl. Add condensed milk gradually, beating well. Beat in egg yolks. Pour into pie shell. Beat egg whites in mixer bowl until soft peaks form. Add cream of tartar and sugar gradually, beating until stiff. Spread over pie sealing to edge. Bake at 350 degrees for 15 minutes or until brown. Yield: 8 servings.

♥ **Approx Per Serving:** Cal 317; Prot 8 g; Carbo 44 g; Fiber <1 g; T Fat 13 g; 37% Calories from Fat; Chol 97 mg; Sod 207 mg.

Rosalyn Adams, Georgia

Lahey Clinic
GLOBAL OUTREACH

Pecan Pie

3 eggs
1/2 cup packed light brown sugar
1 cup dark corn syrup
1 teaspoon vanilla extract
2 tablespoons melted butter
1 cup pecan halves
1 unbaked 9-inch pie shell
1/2 cup whipping cream, whipped

Beat eggs lightly with wire whisk in bowl. Add brown sugar, corn syrup and vanilla, beating until well mixed. Stir in butter and pecans. Pour into pie shell. Bake at 350 degrees for 45 to 50 minutes or until filling is set in center. Cool to room temperature. Serve with whipped cream.
Yield: 8 servings.

♥ Approx Per Serving: Cal 493; Prot 5 g; Carbo 61 g; Fiber 1 g;
  T Fat 27 g; 48% Calories from Fat; Chol 108 mg; Sod 229 mg.

Kassie Kattwinkel, Massachusetts

Ritzy Pecan Pie

3 egg whites
1 teaspoon baking powder
1 cup sugar
1/2 teaspoon vanilla extract
2/3 cup chopped pecans
25 butter crackers, crushed
1 cup whipping cream, whipped

Beat egg whites in mixer bowl until soft peaks form. Add baking powder, sugar and vanilla gradually, beating until stiff peaks form. Fold in pecans and cracker crumbs. Spoon into buttered 9-inch pie plate. Bake at 325 degrees for 30 minutes. Cool. Spread whipped cream over top. Chill for 3 to 4 hours. Yield: 8 servings.

♥ Approx Per Serving: Cal 321; Prot 3 g; Carbo 34 g; Fiber 1 g;
  T Fat 11 g; 31% Calories from Fat; Chol 42 mg; Sod 154 mg.

Robert F. McLellan, Massachusetts

Susan's Pecan Pie

3 eggs, slightly beaten
1/4 cup sugar
1 1/4 cups light corn syrup
1/4 teaspoon salt
1 teaspoon vanilla extract
2/3 cup pecan halves
1 unbaked 9-inch pie shell

Combine eggs, sugar, corn syrup, salt and vanilla in mixer bowl; mix well. Stir in pecans. Spoon into pie shell. Bake at 450 degrees for 10 minutes. Reduce oven temperature to 325 degrees. Bake for 30 minutes longer or until knife inserted near center comes out clean.
Yield: 8 servings.

♥ **Approx Per Serving:** Cal 370; Prot 4 g; Carbo 57 g; Fiber 1 g; T Fat 16 g; 37% Calories from Fat; Chol 80 mg; Sod 253 mg.

Susan Cain, Massachusetts

Shoofly Pie

1 cup flour
2/3 cup packed brown sugar
1 tablespoon (rounded) shortening
1 cup molasses
1 egg, beaten
3/4 cup hot water
1 teaspoon baking soda
1/4 cup boiling water
1 unbaked 9-inch pie shell

Combine flour and brown sugar in bowl; mix well. Cut in shortening until crumbly. Reserve 1/2 cup crumbs. Add molasses, egg and 3/4 cup hot water to remaining crumbs; mix well. Dissolve baking soda in 1/4 cup water. Add to molasses mixture; mix well. Spoon into unbaked pie shell. Sprinkle with reserved crumbs. Bake at 350 degrees for 35 to 40 minutes or until brown. Yield: 8 servings.

♥ **Approx Per Serving:** Cal 365; Prot 4 g; Carbo 66 g; Fiber 1 g; T Fat 10 g; 24% Calories from Fat; Chol 27 mg; Sod 265 mg.

Patricia Eby, M.D., Massachusetts

Nutritional Guidelines

The editors have attempted to present these family recipes in a form that allows approximate nutritional values to be computed. Persons with dietary or health problems or whose diets require close monitoring should not rely solely on the nutritional information provided. They should consult their physicians or a registered dietitian for specific information.

💜 *Abbreviations for Nutritional Profile* 💜

Cal — Calories
Prot — Protein
Carbo — Carbohydrates

Dietary Fiber — Fiber
T Fat — Total Fat
Chol — Cholesterol

Sod — Sodium
gr — gram
mg — milligrams

Nutritional information for these recipes is computed from information derived from many sources, including materials supplied by the United States Department of Agriculture, computer databanks and journals in which the information is assumed to be in the public domain. However, many specialty items, new products and processed foods may not be available from these sources or may vary from the average values used in these profiles. More information on new and/or specific products may be obtained by reading the nutrient labels. Unless otherwise specified, the nutritional profile of these recipes is based on all measurements being level.

- **Artificial sweeteners** vary in use and strength so should be used "to taste," using the recipe ingredients as a guideline. Sweeteners using aspartame (NutraSweet and Equal) should not be used as a sweetener in recipes involving prolonged heating which reduces the sweet taste. For further information, refer to package information.
- **Alcoholic ingredients** have been analyzed for the basic ingredients, although cooking causes the evaporation of alcohol thus decreasing caloric content.
- **Buttermilk**, **sour cream** and **yogurt** are the types available commercially.
- **Cake mixes** which are prepared using package directions include 3 eggs and ½ cup oil.
- **Chicken**, cooked for boning and chopping, has been roasted; this method yields the lowest caloric values.
- **Cottage cheese** is cream-style with 4.2% creaming mixture. Dry-curd cottage cheese has no creaming mixture.
- **Eggs** are all large. To avoid raw eggs that may carry salmonella as in eggnog or 6-week muffin batter, use an equivalent amount of commercial egg substitute.
- **Flour** is unsifted all-purpose flour.
- **Garnishes**, serving suggestions and other optional additions and variations are not included in the profile.
- **Margarine** and **butter** are regular, not whipped or presoftened.
- **Milk** is whole milk, 3.5% butterfat. Lowfat milk is 1% butterfat. Evaporated milk is whole milk with 60% of the water removed.
- **Oil** is any type of vegetable cooking oil. Shortening is hydrogenated vegetable shortening.
- **Salt** and other ingredients to taste as noted in the ingredients have not been included in the nutritional profile.
- If a choice of ingredients has been given, the nutritional profile reflects the first option. If a choice of amounts has been given, the nutritional profile reflects the greater amount.

Index

Curried Lamb, 90
Lazy Man's Leg of Lamb, 90
Noisettes of Lamb with Garlic and Roquefort
    Potato Croquettes, 25
Slow and Easy Lamb, 91
Stuffed Grape Leaves, 15

Mixed Spices or *Baharat*, 70

PASTA
Aglio e Olio, 134
Apricot Kugel, 134
Chicken Parmigiana, 100
Chicken-Spaghetti Casserole, 107
Chinese Fettucini, 133
Fettucini Verde, 133
Italian Clam Sauce, 116
Linguine with Clam Sauce, 117
Linguine with Shrimp and Bread
    Crumbs, 120
Linguine with Smoked Salmon in Caper Cream
    Sauce, 14
Lobster Spaghetti Sauce, 118
Noodle Kugel, 135
Pesto Genovese for Spaghetti, 135
Quigley's Spaghetti Sauce, 87
Spaghetti Pizza, 95
Tasty Tuna Pasta, 115
Timbano Di Pasta with Polpettine, 30
Tortellini with Tomato in Garlic Sauce, 55
Tortellini-Vegetable Salad, 75
Tuna and Pasta Salad, 75
White Wine-Scallop Lasagna, 118

PIES
Cheesecake Pie, 181
Chocolate-Almond-Ricotta Pie, 183
Chupal's Succulent Apple Pie, 181
Cranberry and Coconut Pie, 183
Crunchy Ice Cream Pie, 184
Dutch Apple Pie, 180
Heavenly Pie, 185
Jackie's Bluegrass Chocolate Chip Pie, 184
Key Lime Pie, 29
Old South Lemon Meringue Pie, 185
Pecan Pie, 186
Ricotta Pie, 182
Ritzy Pecan Pie, 186
Shoofly Pie, 187
Susan's Pecan Pie, 187
Swedish Apple Pie, 180

PORK. *See also* Ham; Sausage
Devonshire Pork Filets, 92
Fried Won Tons, 59
Hot and Sour Soup, 38
Pork Hawaiian, 92
Sancocho from the Dominican Republic, 111
Scalloped Potatoes and Pork Chops, 93
Tourtière, 56
Tourtière of Quebec, 56
Vindaloo, 103

SALADS
Broccoli Salad, 76
Casabora Salad, 77
Chargrilled Tuna and Avocado Salad, 37
Duck Salad with Wild Rice, 35
Eggplant Salad, 78
Five-Way Salad, 73
Korean Salad, 79
Mandarin Orange Salad, 79
Marinated Carrots, 78
Mary's Potato Salad, 80
Pineapple Supreme Salad, 74
Three-Bean Salad, 76
Tortellini-Vegetable Salad, 75
Tropical Chicken Salad with Lime
    Dressing, 74
Tuna and Pasta Salad, 75

SALADS, DRESSINGS
Casabora Salad Dressing, 77
Raspberry and Walnut Vinaigrette, 80
Toasted Corn Vinaigrette, 37

SAUCES
Italian Clam Sauce, 116
Linguine with Clam Sauce, 117
Lobster Spaghetti Sauce, 118
Multi-Purpose Tomato Sauce, 136
Pesto Genovese for Spaghetti, 135
Quigley's Spaghetti Sauce, 87
Toasted Almond Sundae Sauce, 22

SAUSAGE
Blueberry and Sausage Breakfast Cake, 138
Carol's Kielbasa, 52
Pepperoni Pie, 54
Teen Bean Bake, 96
Two-Crust Pizza, 96

SHELLFISH
Baked Lobster Savannah, 34
Broiled Crawfish, 117
Car Koay Teow, 119
Carolina Pickled Shrimp, 57
Charred Tuna with Oyster Sauce, 21
Clam Chowder, 43
Crab-Stuffed Chicken Breasts, 109
Crabbies, 47
Gourmet Crab Spread, 48
Individual Lobster Pies, 40
Italian Clam Sauce, 116
Linguine with Clam Sauce, 117
Linguine with Shrimp and Bread Crumbs, 120
Lobster Spaghetti Sauce, 118
Maine Crab Cakes, 16
Mediterranean Seafood Chowder, 32
Mussel Soup, 69
Scalloped Oyster Stuffing, 137
Scallops Chappaquiddick, 122
Seafood Casserole, 122
Shrimp Casserole, 121
Shrimp Creole, 119

Shrimp Puffs, 58
Shrimp Scampi, 121
Tasty Grilled Shrimp, 121
Warm Cape Cod Farmed Bay Scallops with
   Fresh Tomato Extra-Virgin Olive Oil
   Vinaigrette, 33
White Wine-Scallop Lasagna, 118

SIDE DISHES. *See also* Pasta
Baked Rice, 136
Baked Stuffed Pumpkin, 137
Scalloped Oyster Stuffing, 137

SNACKS
Caramel Corn, 59
Chinese Fried Walnuts, 61
Frosted Walnuts, 61
Swedish Nuts, 60
Swedish Pecans, 60

SOUPS
Broccoli and Cheese Soup, 66
Clam Chowder, 43
Cucumber Bisque, 67
Dutch Pea Soup, 39
Fisherman's Pot, 68
Gazpacho, 68
Hot and Sour Soup, 38
Iced Cherry Soup, 44
Lentil Soup, 70
Mediterranean Seafood Chowder, 32
Mussel Soup, 69
Oven Fish Chowder, 67
Parsnip Chowder, 71
Pumpkin Soup, 71
Stateside Cheddar Cheese Soup, 66
Tomato and Pasta Soup, 72
Vegatable Chowder, 72
Vegetable and Beef Soup, 73
Wild Mushroom Soup, 36

VEAL
Anna's Bracciole, 31
Baked Hungarian Veal Goulash, 94
Braised Lemon Veal, 93
Brisket of Veal Roast, 94
Milanesa de Ternera, 95
Tourtière, 56
Veal à la Dray, 44

VEGETABLES
Italian Zucchini Crescent Pie, 132
Macomber Turnip Purée, 131
Sweet Potato and Pineapple Soufflé, 131
Tortellini-Vegetable Salad, 75
Vegetarian Medley, 20
Zucchini Casserole, 132

VEGETABLES, BEANS
Baked Beans, 124
Bean Medley, 124
Black Beans, 20
Green Beans Wrapped in Bacon, 125
Teen Bean Bake, 96
Three-Bean Salad, 76

VEGETABLES, CABBAGE
Grandma's Hungarian Cabbage and Noodle
   Delight, 125
Polish Stuffed Cabbage, 85
Russian Cabbage Pie, 53
Stuffed Cabbage Leaves, 85

VEGETABLES, CARROTS
Carrots Piedmontese, 126
Marinated Carrots, 78
Zesty Carrots, 126

VEGETABLES, EGGPLANT
Cheesy Eggplant Casserole, 127
Eggplant Balls, 127
Eggplant Salad, 78

VEGETABLES, POTATOES
Breakfast Potatoes, 128
Mary's Potato Salad, 80
Mrs. Quigley's Potato Casserole, 128
Noisettes of Lamb with Garlic and Roquefort
   Potato Croquettes, 25
Party Mashed Potatoes, 129
Potato Casserole, 129
Potatoes Dianna, 130

VEGETABLES, SPINACH
Greek Spinach Pie, 54
Ricotta and Spinach Pie, 42
Spinach Balls, 58
Spinach Pie European, 24
Three-Cheese and Spinach Pie, 130

For Additional Copies
Send a check for $12.95 plus $4.00 shipping and handling to:
Lahey Clinic Global Outreach, Philanthropy Office
41 Mall Road
Burlington, Massachusetts 01805-0105
All major credit cards are accepted